SPIRITUAL REFLECTIONS ON THE PATH

Sober Boots

A Collection
by Heather Kopp

The DESK Publishing

Sober Boots: Spiritual Reflections on the Path of Recovery

©2017 Heather Kopp

Published by The DESK Publishing
PO Box 265, Medford, OR 97501
Contact: info@theDESKpublishing.com

ISBN: 978-0-9986737-0-7 paperback
ISBN: 978-0-9986737-1-4 ebook

Cover and interior design Katherine Lloyd, theDESKonline.com
Cover art by Skylar Call

Contents

A Note from the Author

Once upon time, if you had foraged through my messy closet, you would have come upon my small collection of tall boots. And if you happened to peek inside, you'd have discovered they were harboring small bottles of alcohol.

The reason my boots were so thirsty is that they belonged to a secret drunk (that would be me) who thought they made a good hiding place.

For twelve long years, I was determined to keep the truth from my husband and the rest of the world about the real extent of my drinking. Caught in an endless cycle of shame and remorse, I couldn't understand how a good wife and mother, not to mention a writer of books about prayer and parenting, became a closet drunk.

Then one day came surrender. Then came the excruciating step into the light. Then came reaching out for help. Then came a new recovery community and hope. Then came grace and a bigger idea of how God works in the world.

By far the best part of being sober was the opportunity it gave me to share the good news of recovery with others—and thus was born the blog, Sober Boots.

This book is a collection of reflections from that blog over the course of three years, from 2012 to 2015. My sister spearheaded this project, choosing pieces that spoke to the topic of faith and recovery in ways that seemed worthy of retaining for readers. I'm so thankful for her hard work!

The need for this compilation came about after I lost my oldest son Noah in a terrible tragedy in the fall of 2015. I wrote a single post about it, knowing readers would want to know what happened. I was so grateful for the loving response; but I also realized I had made myself vulnerable to feedback that was hurtful. At that point, I turned the blog off or "private."

Since then, I've received a constant flow of requests for permission to view the blog. Some were previous followers who wanted to reread a particular post. Others had read my book, *Sober Mercies: How Love Caught Up With a Christian Drunk*—and they wanted more.

Since I am no longer blogging about recovery, compiling the best of these posts seemed like a good idea. It also frees up the blog for different directions I may want to take in the future.

So much about my life has changed since I wrote these entries. I have gone through a hellish time, friends. I have despaired of wanting to live. I have struggled with my sobriety. I have questioned my purpose on earth and raged at God. And yet, looking back over what now seems a golden time, I haven't changed my mind about anything I wrote.

It's all still true because God is still true.

Best wishes,

Heather

Trapped In a Bathroom
With a Man (and Oprah)

I learned how to scream for help way before I ever got sober.

It happened one summer when Dave and I were staying at a vacation rental house on the Oregon coast. We just so happened to be in the bathroom at the same time—Dave in the shower and me drying my hair—when I heard a very loud crash. Alarmed, I tried to open the bathroom door to investigate. But it wouldn't budge. "Honey?" I called to Dave, "I think we have a problem."

A half hour later, using a metal towel bar as a lever, we had finally managed to pry the upper part of the door open about an inch. Stuffing a towel in the crack to save our progress, we now had a narrow view of our predicament. A sliding door on the closet across from us had inexplicably escaped its track and fallen onto the bathroom door, jamming it shut. The more we tried to force the bath door open, the tighter the closet door wedged us in.

Naturally, this bathroom had no windows. Our cell phones were on the couch in the living room. None of our family or friends knew where we were. We could hardly believe it was happening. We were trapped? In a bathroom?

The only contact we could count on was a cleaning lady who would come to clean *after* we checked out. In five days.

Trying to find the humor in the situation, I pointed out to Dave that we had water, so we wouldn't die. And—hooray—we'd lose a lot of weight. I had brought my *Oprah* magazine into the bathroom with me, so I settled on the toilet (lid down) and started reading aloud to Dave about how to live your best life.

Dave didn't think it was funny. Actually, he'd brought *work* along on vacation. How was he supposed to write devotionals about trusting

God when he was stuck in a bathroom? And then it hit me. My own big problem.

By now, my alcoholism had progressed to the point where I drank copious amounts nightly just to feel normal (a third in front of Dave, the rest in secret, usually guzzled in the *bathroom* with the door locked. *Oh the irony!*). Forget food—without a drink, I'd eventually go into withdrawal. Shakes. Sweating. I'd have to pretend to Dave I had the flu.

Regalvanized by my private terror, I went back to the crack in the door. This time, I realized that I could actually see into the bedroom down the hall. Dave had opened the window a few inches the night before. Even though it was rainy and windy, the people renting the house next door *might* hear us if we yelled loud enough.

Dave thought I should go first. "I think a woman's scream is louder and more alarming. People want to save a screaming woman."

I hesitantly put my face to the crack in the door and . . . I just couldn't do it. "Like, really loud?" I asked Dave, suddenly shy. "At the top of my lungs? But what do I *say*?"

"Try 'help'," Dave said. "The loudest you can. Louder than you've ever screamed in your life."

It took me a while to work up to a Psycho-sized scream. I felt like an actress rehearsing for a horror movie. A few times, I started laughing. But soon I was letting loose with ear piercing screams while Dave huddled in a corner, plugging his ears.

When my throat got sore, I made him take a turn. But asking a grown man to scream for help is like asking him to *run* in the grocery store when you're at the register and realize you forgot something. It's beneath his dignity. He will only stroll.

Given that it was so hard on his pride, I won't even tell you that Dave can scream like a girl. We continued taking turns on and off for at least an hour. Then, my eye to the slit, I thought I saw a motion. A flash of yellow. The people next door were walking past our house!

"You!" I screamed. "You in the yellow shirt! Help! You in the yellow! Help!" The yellow stopped. It came toward the window, but slowly. Hesitant. I kept screaming.

Finally, a woman's face peered in, and we were saved. As soon as she saw our predicament, this heavy-set older lady shoved open the window and climbed through like a firefighter. It was dramatic and hilarious and something I never want to do again.

Recently someone asked me about recovery meetings. What were they really about? And why do I keep going if I don't drink anymore?

"It would take a while to explain," I started. And then I realized it was really very simple. "At first, we go there to ask for help," I told her. "And then we keep going so that when someone else asks for help, we're there to hear them."

There's more to it, to be sure. But asking for help is in some ways the main part, probably because it's the hardest part.

When you remember that addiction is by nature an isolating phenomenon, it's no wonder the solution requires us to move in the opposite direction. For many of us, getting trapped by an addiction is our first experience of something we simply *can't* conquer on our own. We're all but forced to learn how to yell for help.

Of course, even whispering, "I need help," or "I'm stuck and scared," or "I'm trapped by my obsession," is never easy. But in a way, that's the point.

As soon as we give up hope that we can save ourselves from ourselves, as soon as we're willing to put down our pride and cry out for rescue, God shows up in a yellow shirt.

Misery: Not All Pain is Created Equal

Did you ever see that '90s movie, *Misery*? In it, the character played by Kathy Bates holds an author (played James Caan) captive in his own home and mercilessly tortures him. What makes it all so especially creepy is how Bates maintains an overly polite, carefree demeanor even while she's inflicting unspeakable pain.

If I had to choose one word to describe how I felt toward the end of my drinking, it would be that word—"misery."

Every day I woke up feeling sick, exhausted, and afraid. I was like the movie character, tied to a bed while my addiction was smiling sweetly and cooing at me even as it devised new ways to torment me.

And yet. Misery played a part in my salvation. It wasn't until the misery of my drinking eclipsed any imagined misery of sobriety that I was willing to take a chance on recovery. I was convinced that recovery would be unbearably awful—how could it not? But perhaps this new misery might at least be less than the old one. At least it would be different.

I could not have been more wrong. In fact, I have since come to believe that recovering addicts and alcoholics have a greater capacity for joy than those who have never experienced the nightmare of addiction.

That said, sobriety is *not* without pain. Recovery can be difficult, heart-breaking work. But there's a vast difference between *misery* and *pain*. Both hurt. But misery is an extended state of despair where our suffering seems to have no purpose. Pain on the other hand, is a natural part of living and can be put to good purpose. But not unless we stop resisting it and trying to numb it. Only as we embrace our pain—choose to feel it, not pretend to *like* it—can it enlarge our capacity for joy and deepen our compassion for others who suffer.

Why I call myself
a "Christian" drunk

I was around five when my mother whispered the words "alcoholic" and "drunk" in my ear to explain why my step-grandpa was so spitting-mean, smelled funny, and was always falling down his basement stairs.

Later, whenever someone confided to me in a pitying voice, "She's married to an alcoholic," or, "He's a drunk," I nodded in understanding. I knew exactly what kind of shameful assumptions to make.

Becoming a Christian in my teens did nothing to lessen the stigma of alcoholism in my mind. In fact, I'm pretty sure that among the particular crowd I hung out with in my twenties, the phrase "Christian alcoholic," would have been considered an oxymoron.

Needless to say, when in my early thirties I found myself deep in the throes of self-destructive drinking, I felt baffled and ashamed. So I took my drinking underground. I couldn't imagine ever calling myself an alcoholic in front of anyone.

Ironically, today I use the word *drunk* almost as a term of endearment. It's how I and a lot of my friends describe ourselves. And yet, I notice that regular people sometimes flinch with embarrassment when I casually apply the word drunk or alcoholic to myself.

I totally get that. Even when you put the word "recovering" in front of these words, to most people they sound yucky. Icky. Embarrassing.

Recently, while I was working on titles for my book, a search for alternatives didn't get far. "Lush" sounds just as bad as "drunk," and some might say it has an added sleaze factor. When combined with the oft-abused label of "Christian," you get a juxtaposition that not only jars but for some folks sounds like a double negative.

So what's a girl to do? How should I describe myself? Not using *any* labels would be best, of course. But we don't live in that world. Having a shorthand, twitterable way to communicate is a necessity.

For now, I guess I'll try to quit worrying about being misunderstood and simply describe myself using words based on what they mean to *me*.

In my case, "alcoholic" means that I will always be broken in this particular way. "Drunk" doesn't mean inebriated right this minute but a propensity to get that way that I can't for the life of me wish away.

"Recovering" means that these days I understand that when I feel like want a drink, what I'm really craving is something like grace; and "Christian" means that I believe God is making beauty out of my brokenness.

The Bone
of Addiction

Where my husband Dave grew up in Africa as a missionary's kid, the monkeys were loud, dirty, and often a terrible nuisance. Kids from the local tribe sometimes used a proven technique for capturing the critters. They made a trap by wedging a chicken bone horizontally inside of a hollowed out gourd, which they hung from a tree. Soon enough, a monkey would follow its nose to the gourd and reach inside to grab the chicken bone. But the hole in the top of the gourd was big enough for a monkey's hand to fit through, but too small for the bone and the hand to come out together. Once the monkey had latched on to his prize, the village boys would draw near with their nets. Sensing danger, the monkey would screech in terror. And yet, unwilling to let go, he would stay right where he was, holding on to his bone with all his might, until it cost him his life.

Anyone who is an addict can identify with the monkey's dilemma. Clinging is what we do most naturally. Long after it's safe, sane, or even fun anymore, we cling to whatever it is we crave. *Why?* is the mystery.

Once your favorite substance or activity is delivering more pain than pleasure, why hold on? I think it's because letting go *feels* a lot like dying.

Just ask Jerome, a handsome African American man I met when I was in treatment. Jerome had a wife and three little boys at home. He had attended a prestigious college of music on a scholarship, but his schooling, and his once promising future, had both been derailed by his drinking.

I was surprised to learn from Jerome at dinner one night that just prior to coming to treatment, he'd been in the hospital throwing up blood. The doctors had told him frankly that if he didn't stop drinking, he would *die*—and soon. But here's the thing: *He was thinking about it.* In fact, the entire time that I was in treatment with him, he was still debating: *Die—or quit drinking? Quit drinking—or die?*

At first, I thought, *Are you crazy!?* It wasn't until I had wrestled more deeply with my own addiction that I finally understood something. We go to any length to cling to our bone because letting go feels about the same as dying.

In his book, *Grace and Addiction,* Gerald May writes about the addict who is trying to let go of his drug of choice:

> "If the person makes it through . . . to the point of authentically deciding to quit, a profound sense of terror will arise at the prospect of relinquishing the addictive behavior. . . . [The] addiction has become so much a part of the person's life that its relinquishment feels like a death."

In other words, what Jerome really heard that doctor saying was: *Die or ...die?*

I never saw Jerome again, and I don't know if he stayed sober or died.

I thought of him recently when I came across the gospel passage where Jesus told his followers, "If you cling to your life, you will lose it. . . . " Jesus understood that we are clingers by nature. Give us something that looks, tastes, or feels good, and we'll go to almost any length to keep it. In some ways, we are as mysteriously helpless to surrender what's killing us as those monkeys in Africa.

But the good news hiding in this bit of bad news is that we don't have to find the courage or will to surrender on our own. We don't have to let go of our bone first—before we fall to our knees and cry out to God. We can fall first, then let God rescue us from what we can't let go of. If we'll only *admit* that we're too stubborn to save ourselves, we'll discover that God already has.

I like to think of it this way: Because Jesus died a physical death and hung from a tree in my place, I don't have to live a spiritual death, tied to a tree with a bone in my hand.

Hypocrites Like Me

I always hated hypocrites. You know, all those holier-than-thou people who say they believe one thing and then act the opposite.

Ironically, I never *dis*liked hypocrites more than when I was busy being one in secret. If no one *knows* your behavior doesn't match your beliefs, it doesn't really count, right?

Sometimes, it still baffles me how, during all those years when I was drinking alcoholically, I could continue to write and edit Christian books. Publicly, I churned out opinions on things like parenting and prayer, while privately I drank myself past sensibility. As a parent, I came down hard on my kids about drugs and alcohol while I was sneaking a purse loaded with alcohol into their sporting events.

When I first got sober, I was so ashamed of my hypocrisy that I was tempted to cast myself as someone who, over the course of my drinking years, had become spiritually bankrupt, wholly alienated from my faith and only going through the motions. *Pretending.* The story was cleaner that way. And it sounded right.

But as my husband gently pointed out, it wasn't the whole truth. Yes, my relationship with God suffered significantly as a result of my addiction. And yes, I'd grown increasingly disillusioned with a faith that couldn't seem to save me. But a very real part of me also continued to care deeply about my relationship with God. I prayed. I read His words and listened for His voice. I hoped He could still use me somehow for good.

I mention this not as a defense, or to mitigate my guilt, but because I know how easy it is to want to believe that only *one* thing is true about a person at a time. (Isn't this why we're stunned when a respected leader is caught in a web of lies?)

But the truth is that each of us is more than our most current failure. And the good, if uncomfortable news, is that God doesn't use any of us because we're worthy, but because He is good. Not only does he work *in spite of* our shortcomings, He often works *through them*.

Besides, given the gross, seemingly unfixable flaws in human nature, it makes sense that God would get a little desperate. If He wasn't willing to use broken people and hypocrites like me, He'd have no choice but to put us all in a free bin at His next garage sale. (I'm only joking about this last part.)

How to Live
a Double Life

In my last piece, I wrote about being a hypocrite. I concluded that while we may want only one thing to be true about a person at a time, most of us are a bundle of paradoxes. And while God asks us to reach for wholeness, He's clearly not averse to working through our brokenness.

This is good news. But the implications can seem a little troubling to some people. I mean, if I really *was* a person who genuinely wanted to love and serve God during those years when I was a secret drunk, *how* did I live for so long with such a split heart? How did I *manage* it? How does that *work*?

One of the most surprising answers I've arrived at is this: *One day at a time.*

In recovery, "one day at a time" is a positive prescription for how to stay sober over the long haul. Ironically, it's also how this drunk managed to stay drunk for so many years. As long as I could say every day with utter sincerity, "Dear God, I can't believe I drank again last night. Help me quit!" I could keep myself from seeing the bigger picture of what had become of my life.

I think it's a common pattern among addicts of all kinds. By living each day in sincere regret about our most recent failure, we can feel good about feeling guilty without having to acknowledge the terrible truth of the chasm dividing our heart.

Of course, another reason that I could live a double-life for so long—versus *fully* abandoning God for the bottle—has absolutely nothing to do with me. It was because God never abandoned me. Even in the midst of my faithlessness, God was faithful. Even as I ran, my bottle clutched tightly to my chest, He relentlessly pursued me, His love leaping ahead of better judgment.

Sober Boots

These days, my heart still suffers small fractures and cracks, created in moments of fear, selfishness, and compromise. But the difference now is that every morning I wake up and pray, "Thank you God that I *didn't* drink last night! Please keep me sober today." And often I catch myself *hoping* to catch a glimpse of the bigger story my life is telling, one word at a time.

Scary People
in Birkenstocks

et's face it, I got a few things backward. I was supposed to become a Christian, get free of the bondage of sin, and go on to make other disciples. What I did instead was go on to become a secret drunk.

Of course, that was never my plan. As a young Christian in my early twenties, I rarely imbibed, I went to church twice a week, I joined small groups, I believed all the right things about God (or so I thought), and I carried my Bible with me everywhere—even to get my hair cut.

But there was a problem when it came to the whole making disciples thing. How could I talk to people about God when I was so leery of anyone who seemed different than me? Having paid close attention to how my crowd dressed, talked, and voted, I could spot this scary otherness a mile away. I remember getting really nervous around people who wore Birkenstocks, frequented health food stores, voted Democrat, or cared too much about the environment.

Since I lived in Eugene, Oregon, home to legions of hippies, ninety percent of the people I met were "other." I could have viewed the fields as ripe for harvest, especially since I'm pretty sure my only real interest in anyone "other" back then was to proselytize them. But mostly I stuck close to my conservative church crowd and stared out at the world from behind its skirts. I was content to fervently pray on Wednesday nights for all those people out there who needed to find God in the same way I had.

When I got into recovery in my early forties, I found myself for the first time surrounded by an array of people who were, by most measures, not like me. And yet, I had never been so warmly welcomed by a group of strangers. Here, no one cared how you dressed, where you worked, what you believed, or how you voted. Here, I was finally stripped of all my convenient labels for others and of ways of describing myself as anything other than a garden variety drunk. It was the worst and best thing that ever happened to me.

Still, I was baffled. I mean, how could a bunch of addicts and alcoholics have managed to create the kind of loving and loyal community that I had tried and failed to find in so many Christian groups over the years? But desperate to stay sober, I set aside my wonder and dove in. And there, among the beautifully broken, I began learning how to be part of a Christ-like community. I began, too, to understand what it means to depend on God's grace instead of just believe in it.

Today, some of my closest friends used to snort coke, wake up with one stranger after another, and dance on tabletops in bars.

Today, I love the church we attend. It's not a club where I feel comfortably cloistered and must learn how to conform. Instead, it's an open community that reaches out to people of all kinds, receiving them in any condition with open arms.

Today, my bafflement about finding community in recovery has passed. I think I get it now, and I think it's really pretty simple. It's definitely something Jesus understood: People bond more deeply over shared brokenness than they do over shared beliefs.

Drinking at Dave

My grown son Nathan sent me an article about a famous baseball player with a history of addiction who had recently relapsed with alcohol.

My first thought was, *Why would someone with so much at stake do something so stupid?* And then I caught myself. Being famous doesn't make you less of an alcoholic, it just makes your failures more public.

My second thought was, *I wonder who this guy was mad at?*

I scanned the article. Sure enough, he attributed his "moment of weakness" to "a personal reason involving a family member."

I had been sober a little more than five months when Dave and I took a trip to New York City. We had so many groovy things to do that I didn't go to any recovery meetings or spend my usual time with God in the mornings. By now, I figured I had this thing down.

The day before we left, I got angry at Dave about something dumb. And I stayed angry, stewing in my resentment. On the first leg of our flight home, we put the argument on hold for lack of privacy. But I knew we had a layover in Minneapolis, and I was certain Dave would want to find a quiet corner where he could finally beg me to forgive him.

Instead, as we deplaned, he suggested that we go our separate ways and meet back up at the next gate. He was tired of my glaring at him.

The gall! I stormed off in the opposite direction. *He knows I'm angry and hurting,* I fumed. *He knows airports are dangerous for me. He knows I might drink. Obviously, he doesn't care!*

I marched into a bar determined to drink at Dave. I ordered and downed two enormous glasses of Chardonnay. Then I popped in some spearmint gum and headed to find our gate.

When he approached me in the waiting area, I made a smart

remark. Right off, he asked if I'd been drinking. "Of course not!" I said, pretending outrage. "How could you even ask such a thing?"

But once we got onto the plane, I reconsidered. The whole point was to punish Dave by drinking, since I knew my sobriety was precious to him. When the attendant came down the aisle with the drink service, I saw my opportunity.

"I'll have a glass of white wine," I announced, reaching across Dave to hand her my credit card.

"What are you *doing*?" Dave asked, obviously alarmed.

"I'm having a drink. Do you *mind*?" The flight attendant hesitated, then poured my wine. I flipped down the tray table and placed the cup and mini-bottle in front of me. I started to sip it slowly.

Dave turned away so he wouldn't have to watch.

I hated myself. As I sipped from the cup, salty tears slipped down my face and ran into my wine, and I drank them.

Still, after we got home, I made sure our fight lasted for another two days. Not because I wasn't sorry, but so that my stupid relapse could last a little longer and I could keep drinking.

On the third day, sanity returned. Remorseful and mortified, I begged Dave's forgiveness. I went to a meeting and admitted what I'd done. To this day, when I celebrate my sobriety birthday in September instead of April, I regret that relapse.

I ran across a news story once about a woman in Texas who took revenge on an ex-boyfriend by stealing all of his pet goldfish (koi?). The boyfriend alerted police, but by the time the cops arrived at her home, she had pan-fried and eaten the fish, all but one, which lay in the pan nicely crisped, evidence for the police.

I couldn't believe it. What was she thinking? Why would she do that to herself? She should have tricked the boyfriend into eating his own fish. Or at least fried them at his house and left them in the pan for him to see.

Of course, when I drank at Dave in the Minneapolis airport, I did pretty much the same thing. *Take that, Buster!*

But I was the one who ate the fish.

In recovery we're fond of the saying: "Holding onto resentment is like taking poison and waiting for the other person to die." I guess taking revenge on someone by hurting yourself is like eating the other person's goldfish and waiting for it for to taste yummy.

You don't have to be a celebrity or a drunk to make either mistake.

Porta Potty Prayers

I met Hector early in sobriety. He's Hispanic, mid-twenties, small in stature, and handsome in a sweet way. One day, he told me in halting English how grateful he was to God to be sober and free.

He told me he works construction. Everyone at his work drinks and does drugs. He used to do the same. In fact, he often used the on-site port-a-potty to smoke marijuana and slug hard liquor.

He still spends a lot of time in the port-a-potty, he said. Only now he goes there to beg God to help him stay sober. "There is a tiny mirror inside of the port-a-potty door," he explained. "I go and look in the mirror and I say, 'Hector, you no want to drink or do drugs. Think about your wife. Think about your baby.' And I ask for God to help me."

And then he added, "I make you laugh maybe. But that port-a-potty is my sanctuary."

His words didn't make me laugh. They pierced my soul.

In the coming months, I heard some version of Hector's simple refrain again and again: *I cried out for help, and God answered me. Now I rely on Him every day to keep me sober.*

Of course, I came into recovery thinking I knew all about God. I was pretty sure that I could have outlined a Bible study on trusting God for anyone, including Hector.

So why did I want what Hector and so many others had?

One day, it dawned on me that most of my new friends in recovery had arrived at their faith in the opposite way that I had. I started out with a prescribed set of biblical beliefs that told me what to *think* about God, and then I tried to put these ideas into action.

But many of them had begun with nothing except a desperate need to stay sober. They decided to rely on God, and as he proved himself trustworthy, they came to conclusions about his power and love based on their experience.

The result? I had a working knowledge of Scripture. But many of my fellow alcoholics had a more biblical grasp on God's grace and goodness than I did.

It was a staggering revelation.

Maybe you can relate. It's easy to get so focused on what we know in our head that we lose track of what we can only discover with our hearts.

It's easy to forget that any place we choose to plead, cry out, and beg God for help—even a port-a-potty—becomes in that moment a sanctuary.

Why God Can't Be Trusted

Today I heard from a friend in Oregon I've known for decades. Kim and her husband have always been wonderful Christian parents who pray regularly for their kids. Now she tells me that her oldest son—who I've known since he was two—is a heroin addict living on the streets in Portland.

I won't try to describe her anguish. We've all heard these stories. Some of us have lived them. Parents pray faithfully for their children's safety and well-being. And then something truly horrible and tragic happens. So why bother praying? Can God *really* be trusted?

I used to think so. For many years, a critical part of my faith hinged on the idea that my prayers would influence God to intervene in the world on behalf of those I love. If I just prayed hard enough, often enough, and made sure to throw in plenty of thanksgivings before and after, God would come through.

When He didn't, I pretended not to notice, maybe because it felt awkward and embarrassing to point out to God how much He had let me down. Or I told myself that God had declined to do my will for good and loving reasons I might understand later. Or I told myself that I just hadn't prayed with enough faith and fervor to move God to act on my behalf. Or, especially during my drinking years, I concluded that *of course* God doesn't answer prayers from drunks like me. But would God punish other people just because I prayed for them and he needed to say no to me? It was all very confusing.

Something I haven't mentioned yet is that I'm also the mother of an alcoholic. By the time I got into recovery in my early forties, my oldest son was in deep trouble with drinking and drugs. For years I anguished. And I prayed. I offered up all kinds of affirmations predicting God's help—as if pretending my faith was firm could make it less like the jello it really was.

One morning, I got a phone call from my son. He was in such a dark, scary place that I had no idea what to say to him. And every word I did say sounded hollow. Tragedy seemed imminent. If he didn't die of an overdose or a car accident, I feared he would take his life.

After we hung up, I couldn't help wondering how long he could hang on. Or how long *I* could. Sitting there in my office chair, cradling the phone, something about this whole prayer-of-faith formula—at least as I'd been practicing it—began to enrage me. I just couldn't bear the responsibility of praying hard enough to save my son anymore. Neither could I deny any longer the betrayal I felt about the very idea that I had to twist God's arm harder to make Him care more.

I began to cry. More truthfully, I wailed. I told God that I was sick and tired of feeling like I was being forced to repeatedly watch my child about to fall off a high cliff, knowing that no matter how fast I got there, it would not be soon enough to catch him. And then I felt myself being led where no mother wants to go—deep into the territory of worst-case scenario. In my imagination, and more important, in my heart, my son died. I cried and keened and wrestled with God.

I don't know how long this went on, but I finally arrived somewhere outside of and beyond my faith. For the first time, I realized that I could not trust God to keep my son—or anyone's son—out of harm's way. Because God can't be trusted to deliver a particular outcome. He can only be trusted with, or in spite of, any outcome. He can only be trusted no matter what. But "no matter what" is a dagger to a mother's heart, because it means that your only hope is to surrender all hope. "No matter what" is a place you never hope to go.

Now I saw clearly that it would have to be everything or nothing. Either I trusted God with my son's entire life (and his death if it came) in a way that surpassed my understanding of what is good, or I didn't trust Him at all.

That morning, I decided to place my son and all my hope in the hands of a God whose love is so vast and incomprehensible that it encompasses everything—even tragedy. I decided to put my hope in a

God so good that one day, if only in eternity, even death and suffering will make some kind of beautiful sense.

Of course, I didn't resolve all my questions about prayer that day. But something shifted. I determined that I would no longer pray to a God who was a puppet on a string—His will being tugged this way or that, depending on how hard people prayed or if they managed to stay awake.

I still pray. I still ask God to intervene. I still think that kind of prayer has a place. Why else would "Help me!" fall from our lips so often and so naturally? In fact, my entire recovery from alcoholism rests on my belief that God *does* intervene, that He can and will do for me what I can't do for myself.

A couple weeks ago my son celebrated four years of continuous sobriety. He's a walking miracle, working hard on his own recovery, and every day I'm grateful. But the way I see things now, he probably wouldn't be where he is today if he hadn't hit that terrible "bottom" I had been begging God to save him from.

I keep this in mind today as I pray for Kim's son. Really, I'm not just praying, I'm pleading. I'm begging. Not because I think God needs to be persuaded to care more, but because I know He already does.

The Trouble
with Free Will

My piece about trusting God *with* outcomes instead of *for* them generated a lot of response. Among the comments was this one:

"Free will is amazing to have, but so frustrating to fight against. It will always trump our prayers. We serve a loving God who will never force Himself upon us, or upon people we pray for if they don't want Him. Damn you, free will, I love you."

Isn't that last line just perfect? On the one hand, we're so grateful for the gift of choice. And yet, speaking for myself, I have often wished God would take the gift back and exchange it for something more cooperative, something that doesn't make me want to pull my hair out. Imagine how many parents whose kids are in deep trouble with alcohol or drugs would love to revoke their child's free will. (How does God manage to restrain Himself every day as He watches *us*?)

Free will is one of the most baffling aspects of our self-destructive obsessions. I mean, if I really do get to choose for myself, then why can't I just *decide* to stop?

But of course, it's not that simple. Which raises an important question: Do we *lose* free will when we become addicted? It sure *feels* that way. At least it did for me when I was still drinking. But I think it's better to say that our will gets hijacked and divided by the power of addiction.

Once you determine that you truly no longer want to drink (or, _____, fill in your own blank here), and then you still do, you're acting against your own will. The one of you has split into two. You start to sound like the apostle Paul when he wrote:

> "I do not understand what I do. For what I want to do I do
> not do, but what I hate I do. And if I do what I do not want to
> do, I agree that the law is good. As it is, it is no longer I myself
> who do it, but it is sin living in me. . . . For I have the desire
> to do what is good, but I cannot carry it out. For I do not do
> the good I want to do, but the evil I do not want to do—this
> I keep on doing. Now if I do what I do not want to do, it is
> no longer I who do it, but it is sin living in me that does it . . .
> What a wretched man I am!" (from Romans 7).

Did you follow all that? I have no idea if Paul was an addict, as
some conjecture. But it sure sounds like he's saying here, "Sin made
me do it. It wasn't really *me*."

Reading Paul's words, I can't help thinking again of my friend's
heroin-addicted son.

One recent weekend, she and her husband took some family and
friends to Portland and spent the entire day searching for their son
among the homeless and drug-addled. When they finally found him.
"he looked sick and emaciated," she reports. "We hardly recognized
him."

He refused to come home. *Think about this.* He wouldn't come
home—to love and safety; to a wife ready to forgive and support him;
to a five-year-old daughter who hasn't seen her daddy for months and
misses him every day.

I think it's safe to say that part of my friend's son, the part she
knows and loves, desperately wants to come home. But another part,
the addicted part, is winning, for now.

Understanding that addiction divides us against ourselves also
helps to explain why it is so incredibly powerful. How do you win a
battle with addiction when every ounce of self-will and self-reliance
that you muster for the fight is shared by the addict in you, too . . .
because you share the same will? Obviously, if our will itself is divided,
will-power or trying harder is not the answer.

Where is hope then? *Wretched girl that I am!* Paradoxically, hope
is found in becoming so hopeless that we're finally ready to turn our

entire will over to God, circumventing the vicious tug-of-war we have been having with ourselves. Only as we use this wonderful, terrible gift of free choice for it's greatest purpose—surrender—do we finally find freedom.

Despite all the pain I hear in people's stories, I find that I am grateful for free will. As much as it sets us up for heartache, it also invites us to hope. It means that as long as any of us is alive, we can still say *yes* to rescue. *Yes* to grace. *Yes* to coming home.

In the Land
of Hungry Ghosts

hadn't been sober for long before the emptiness I had escaped through alcohol returned. If you're human, you know what I'm talking about. That nagging sense of soul discontent. That hollow feeling that tells you life is not enough, and neither are you. That nebulous craving for more of something you cannot name.

You would think the solution to this kind of spiritual emptiness would be obvious—God. I used to think so too. I grew up hearing about the cross-shaped hole in everyone's soul that can only be filled by Jesus. After I became a Christian, I also picked up on the notion that I *should* feel fulfilled. How could my soul thirst for more when I had a "river of life" flowing out of me?

Since I *did* thirst for more, I decided I just wasn't spiritual enough. I wasn't trying hard enough. Eventually, alcohol helped me numb the pain and stop caring so much.

One day after I'd gotten into recovery, I came upon an article about the hungry ghosts of another religion. Especially in Asia, many followers believe that people who are too greedy or envious in this life become "hungry ghosts" in the next. Typically, these departed souls are depicted with necks too skinny to swallow and grotesquely enormous bellies. Their fate is to wander the "realm of hungry ghosts," perpetually voracious but unable to satisfy their appetites.

It's easy to see why hungry ghosts are so often associated with addiction, isn't it? Every summer throughout Asia, people celebrate "hungry ghost festivals." Hoping to appease their greedy, departed ancestors, families provide entertainment and lay out gifts of food. Sometimes, these offerings include paper replicas of houses, cars, or other valuable items, which are then ceremonially burned. Descriptions of this custom use words like "appease" and "placate," since you can't possibly *satisfy* a hungry ghost. You can only pretend to relieve its suffering by giving it food you know it can't consume, or by offering it something that looks like what it craves, but is only a copy of the real thing.

At first, this ceremony struck me as silly, and from the ghost's perspective, more cruel than consoling. But then it dawned on me how closely this practice mirrors our addictive impulse.

Speaking for myself, I tend to interface with the world like a greedy hungry ghost. I can't get enough of what looks good, feels good, or even slightly resembles the shape of what I imagine I crave. And yet, the drink or romance or fame or fortune I seek can no more fill my emptiness than a picture of a car can drive me where I want to go.

At some point in my recovery, I came to believe that addiction to any substance or activity is a substitute for the spiritual sustenance our soul really craves. But what I still couldn't understand was why I had so often felt empty in the past, even before I ever started drinking and *while* I was trying my hardest to pursue God.

Now, I think the key phrase in that statement is "trying my hardest." And now, I wonder if it was God I was really pursuing or just something to make me feel good.

This shift in my perspective came about after I picked up Gerald May's book, *The Awakened Heart,* where he wrote:

We were never meant to be completely fulfilled; We were meant to taste it, to long for it, and to grow toward it. . . . The secret to living life as it was meant to be is . . . .to befriend our yearning instead of avoiding it, to live into our longing rather than trying to resolve it, to enter the spaciousness of our emptiness instead of trying to fill it up.

After years of feeling like my heart was always emptying faster than I could fill it, his words startled me. Could it be true? Could it be that what I needed wasn't something to fill that inner empty space, but the courage to leave it empty?

I began to experiment. When I felt especially discontent, instead of reaching for something to eat or pursuing a compulsive distraction,

Sober Boots

Handwritten margin notes: "Or if I still not trying to fill that space — Would God fill it if only for the...", "If so why would that empty space return?"

I sat in a chair, lit a candle, and tried to welcome my feelings of emptiness. After a while, I realized this sensation didn't hurt so much as it felt like God was gently tugging on my soul.

In the months that followed, the more I was willing to claim this longing for God, the more that inner ache began to seem like evidence of His presence instead of His absence. I began to understand that God's abiding or fullness only *feels* like emptiness to me sometimes because it's nothing like the numbness I so regularly mistake for satisfaction.

As humbling and crushing as our compulsions can be, I think they also serve a purpose. They remind us of our ravenous appetite for spiritual sustenance. They remind us that we are desperate for nothing so much as we are desperate for God. They remind us that when we think we want a drink or a drug (or, _____ fill in your own blank here), what we really crave is more of what we already *have*.

So forget hungry ghosts. We have been given a Holy Ghost. And while it's true that presence within us makes us yearn for even *more*, it is also proof of the promise that one day we will become fully united with his Spirit. Since we have this hope, we don't despair when temptation comes to town, flashing its cheap wares. Instead, we recognize the worthlessness of the paper cars and houses, the food and money.

In the act of noticing what is false, we burn up the lie of addiction. We offer the ashes back to God as a gift. And in the smoky air that lingers, we sense the barest hint of the wholeness that will one day be ours.

Two Words
I Need to Hear

opposite of opposite of a (period of turmoil in real life) wordh.ppo.com 2/2/21

opp of drama; peace, tranquility; content quiet silence patience composure

Afriend alerted me to a short YouTube clip of an old Bob Newhart show that God used to speak to me. *Loudly.* You could even say rudely. It's very funny, so it's made the rounds; but if you haven't seen it yet, you need to. (Plus, this won't make as much sense unless you see it. Search for: Bob Newhart, Stop It clip).

Yep. A lot of our problems could be solved by those two simple words: *Stop it!* Watching this woman respond to Bob Newhart's rebuke reminded me of all the drama I used to create around small events in order to make them big enough to drink over.

But getting hooked on drama isn't just something that happens to addicts or alcoholics. It happens to people. And forgive me, but women are the worst offenders, which is why we talk about "drama queens" and not "drama kings."

Not long ago, I was explaining to a friend over coffee that I hadn't had a period (sorry, guys) in several months. "I think I might be in early menopause," I told her. "Wow," she said, with genuine concern. "I went through that a few years ago. It was traumatic to think I couldn't have a baby now."

"That's what I've heard," I said. "But I haven't decided yet if I'm going to have a crisis over it or not."

We both laughed at the joke. → *for attention*

But, seriously, why do we act this way? I'm sure it's partly just human nature. We're attracted to what makes us feel part of a bigger, more exciting story. Drama is what makes TV and movies entertaining and keeps us on the edge of our seats. But since life is rarely like the movies, we look for ways to feel alive, to feel central to the action.

non-effected or moved by drama

Sometimes, it doesn't even matter if it's good or bad, so long as something is *happening*. Plus, if something important is happening to *us*, or even to someone near us, it makes us feel important. All eyes are on the woman in crisis.

Of course, I'm not minimizing legitimate trauma and suffering. But in recovery, we tend to view all drama with a wary eye. The reason it makes us nervous is that it tends to get us wound up and stressed out and next thing you know we want to calm down, be soothed and comforted. And guess where that leads?

Last week I rushed into a cafe to meet a friend, late and flustered. When she asked how I was doing, I downloaded for five minutes. "My life is going to be chaos until March, at least," I explained, feeling a little self-important. *Oh the drama!*

She looked at me quietly for a moment. Then she asked serenely, "Why have you already *decided* that your life will be chaos? It doesn't have to be unless you decide that it will be."

She was right. *Stop it!* She was saying, *Just stop it!* But here's the good news. I heard her. I heard myself. And more importantly, I heard God.

I'm sort of making a joke of it here, but this drama business is actually serious stuff, especially for people on a spiritual path. When we get hooked on chaos and upheaval, we are reaching for meaning and significance in circumstances instead of God. And when we beg, steal, and borrow trouble, we buy into the illusion that the world revolves around us.

Today, I want to choose peace. I want to relax in God's arms at the very moment I could choose to freak out. I want to bring calm into the lives of others, not a spoon to stir up trouble. I want to *Stop it*.

But now, I'm worried. Now that I've written this, every time I find myself lathered up about something that doesn't deserve soap, I just know I'm gonna hear God say, *Stop it! Just, Stop it!*

Only in my head, I'm gonna picture Bob Newhart as God. And that feels like a problem.

On Days When
I Start to Drown

When I was young, my mother sent me to the local YMCA for swim lessons. Eventually, I was ready to move up from being a Guppy in the kiddie pool to become a Flying Fish in the adult pool. But first, I had to pass a test in the deep end.

They call it "dead man's float." For five minutes, I was supposed to do nothing but lie there and drift.

But I didn't do *dead* well. Or maybe the words "dead man" scared me. Every time, I'd panic and start to dog paddle. I couldn't just relax and float to save my life, which was the whole point of the exercise.

Eventually, my instructor gave up and moved me up to Flying Fish anyway. But not before she told me that I'd be sorry someday when I got stranded in the middle of the ocean.

That hasn't happened yet.

Then again, maybe it has. Toward the end of my drinking, that's how I felt. Ten years of thrashing about trying to save myself had left me exhausted, gulping water, and sinking fast. Right up until the minute God saved me, I knew I was going to drown.

I think this is why God loves the last minute. By then, there's no chance that we'll mistake his rescue for our own efforts.

These days, I'm still learning how to swim in the deep end of life without reaching for alcohol. I have to do my part—go to meetings, call other alcoholics, work on my program. But sometimes, I also have to trust God to hold me up when life gets scary or water starts to shoot up my nose.

Once, I heard a woman in a recovery meeting say: "Remember, you can always flip over on your back and float."

I knew what she meant. In the middle of a stressful day, it's easy to imagine that if you just swim faster, just try harder, you'll be able to manage better. But what if instead you turned on your back, so to speak, and let go of everything you can't control anyway?

As a spiritual practice, it's easier said than done.

For me, sometimes it helps to think of my mother. In addition to those swim lessons, she and my step-dad often took us kids to the YMCA on Friday nights for family swim. My mother would spend the entire hour gently bobbing on her back, the extra weight she bemoaned now buoying her up, the water in her ears muffling the shrieks of children playing all around.

She told us she sometimes napped.

The older I get, the less I believe her. But the more I want to be like that.

Heed the Niggle

Today the niggle keeps telling me to write about my hairdresser, a gorgeous waif of a girl with big curly brown hair and beautiful gypsy eyes.

At first I resist, intent on writing something that sounds like more fun. But when the niggle persists.

Every woman knows how hard it is to move to a new town and find a new hairdresser. I'm monogamous about mine, meaning I stick to one forever. So when we moved to a new town, I cringed, picked the salon closest to my house, and hoped for luck. And I struck gold.

Michelle's salon was located in a Victorian style house in our old-fashioned neighborhood. A salon of her own like this had long been her dream, and her husband had helped make it happen. It was cozy and smartly designed. Her large sheep dog named Rosie was always lying nearby and Michelle was always trying to sweep around her. She didn't have kids, so Rosie was her baby.

I went to see Michelle every five weeks for more than two years. We discovered we were exactly the same age, only a couple of months apart. She was a deep thinker and we loved to talk. As happens, we became close. When I got into recovery, I shared all about that, too.

During the second year of my visits, Michelle's husband had an affair. She was heartbroken and divorce quickly followed. Eventually, she got a new boyfriend, and then they broke up. She got depressed. She confided that she was in therapy. Michelle was very close to her mother, and I was glad to see them take a mother-daughter trip to Italy that summer. She came back wearing the coolest jeans I'd ever seen. Like I said, this girl was a stunner. More rounds with the boyfriend ensued. And then Rosie the dog got cancer and had to be put down, a devastating blow.

One day, Michelle asked me if I was still doing those recovery meetings. Of course, I told her. I love them. She went on to confess that she was pretty sure she had a drinking problem. She'd been drinking every night til she passed out and couldn't stop. The on-off boyfriend had a drinking and drug problem, too. She was thinking maybe sometime she could go with me to one of my meetings.

"I'd love that!" I told her. "Absolutely. Cool!" I rattled off some of my regular days and times. When I left the salon, I invited her to call me and we'd go together. "You have my number?" I asked. "Duh," I added, "Of course you do. You only call me before every appointment."

She didn't call that week. In the coming days, it occurred to me that I should make it easier for her. Since I'd been in recovery, I was learning to stop saying to people, "Call me," and instead say, "I'll call *you*," and then follow through.

So I decided to drop a note by her salon with some encouraging words and a meeting schedule. Only then, I got busy. And after a few weeks, it made more sense to just plan on re-issuing the invitation when I saw her for my next appointment. This time, I'd make sure we set a firm date for coffee and a meeting.

The Saturday before my Monday hair appointment, I got a call from the salon to confirm. Only it was a man, and he said he'd have to reschedule me with another person. I was confused. "But where's Michelle?"

"She's not doing hair anymore."

"What do you mean? She *owns* the salon."

And then it hit me. "Did something happen?" I asked, suddenly terrified. No answer.

"She took her life, didn't she?" I knew. I just did.

"Yeah," he said, sounding relieved that I'd guessed. "She left a note. Intentional overdose."

I hung up the phone and thought I would throw up. Having had more than my fair share of experience with suicides, I knew better than to blame myself for her death. But regret? You bet. Rage? I wailed. *Why didn't I follow through? Why didn't I do what I felt so strongly prompted to?* The irony felt unbearable—that I had been way too busy with my new life in recovery to follow up with someone who had taken a risk to reach out to me for help.

I couldn't quit thinking about Michelle's mom, whom I'd met a couple times. Oddly enough, I also couldn't quit thinking about the new stray dog Michelle had recently taken in and how no one would be able explain to it what happened or help it to understand. I think I identified with the dog because I couldn't make sense of it either.

Today I have another hairdresser who's become a good friend. But I can't take that seat and have her pull the cape over me without thinking of Michelle. And the slight edge of hope I'd heard in her voice when she asked about "those meetings." And how she probably had to work hard just to ask that once, and didn't have the emotional strength to pursue it further, to call and invite herself all over again.

It's sort of ironic that I had a niggle today to write about a time when I ignored one. So maybe I'm making progress.

And maybe the only point of this is to remind you that some of us are not okay. We appear to have a good life, we're successful and loved by plenty of people, but inside we're so hurt and tired that we can't hold onto hope.

So listen to your heart. Heed the niggle. Because you just never know.

(And yes, niggle is a real word).

Redeeming
My Regrets

Friday, I had coffee with a good friend who had read, *Heed the Niggle*. "I was glad to hear you didn't blame yourself for Michelle's suicide," she told me. "But how did you manage not to?"

Then Saturday morning brought a heartbreaking email from a mom: "I too, ignored a niggle because it was too implausible," she wrote. "My alcoholic daughter died at the age of 34—but I really didn't think it could happen. I am learning to live with myself. That's about it."

I love that kind of honesty. Both of their responses seemed to invite a follow up: *Heed the niggle, yes. But how do you handle the guilt when you realize you didn't?*

I mentioned that suicide wasn't new to me. My father, who suffered from severe manic-depression, as well as drug addiction, spent most of my childhood in and out of mental hospitals, missions, and halfway houses. He attempted suicide too many times to count.

Through it all, I still thought of myself as a daddy's girl. I never stopped hoping he'd get better. When he was forty-seven, he finally succeeded at taking his life.

Despite so many close calls in the past, I was caught off guard. For years afterward, I wrestled with guilt. *What could I have done or said differently?*

Since his death, another family member committed suicide and another close to me has threatened or attempted suicide several times. Two other people I considered friends succeeded in taking their lives. Given my history, and my failure to heed the niggle about Michelle, it's fair to wonder how I could have *not* felt horribly guilty about her death.

I should clarify that at first, I did. I was sick with guilt, devastated by my failure as a friend. And had I still been drinking, I think I would have stayed that course. I would have gladly soaked in tubs of guilt for weeks, made the tragedy all about me, and used the drama as an excuse to drink.

But by then, I was beginning to understand that I was not just powerless over alcohol, but over other people and their choices.

As a good friend pointed out, to imagine Michelle's life or death hinging on me would be a gross exaggeration of my power. She was right.

Meanwhile, it was dawning on me that to claim responsibility or even partial culpability in Michelle's death would reinforce a lie that had haunted me ever since my dad died: *If someone you love commits suicide, obviously you didn't love them well enough.*

It's a convincing lie because we can always think of something we could or should have done differently. I found myself praying that Michelle's mother wouldn't buy into that lie. I knew that I no longer could.

Early in recovery, I came across a quote by author Sister Mary Beckett about the difference between guilt and true contrition. "Guilt means you go on belaboring and . . . beating your breast and being ego-fixated," she wrote. Contrition means that you're "willing to forgo the pleasures of guilt."

How dare she call guilt pleasurable? I thought. *It's painful and awful!* Now I think it depends on the kind of guilt we're talking about.

Guilt that comes from doing something you know is wrong is a gift from God, an invitation to change course. And it's never pleasurable.

But the kind of guilt Beckett was referring to is the kind related to failures in the past that we can't go back and change today. The kind that, paradoxically, we luxuriate in as a form of self-punishment so that we can feel better for having paid a price for our mistakes. We tell ourselves that we deserve to suffer, but on some level our suffering is self-serving and helps no one.

I understand that brand of guilt. For much of my life I was deluded into believing that guilty feelings in and of themselves had spiritual value, that they were a virtue.

Wouldn't God want me to be racked with guilt? Doesn't that say something good about me? Not really. In fact, it means that I am putting more faith in the effectiveness of my feelings of regret than I am in the effectiveness and power of forgiveness.

On a more practical level, I'm discovering that when I am busy indulging in guilt, I miss the flow of grace into my life through which God can redeem the things I regret. When I take perverse pleasure in hoarding my mistakes, wounds, and losses, how can God turn them into something good?

Sure, we try to heed the niggle when it comes, we try to let God work through us to help someone. But it would be short-sighted to imagine that any mistake I make is more powerful than God's ability to redeem.

I Can't Help It
If I'm Right

Nor long ago I was at a women's recovery meeting where we passed a basket and each of us drew a slip of paper printed with one of the slogans we often use, such as, "One day at a time." The plan was to go around the room and each woman would share her phrase and what it meant to her.

But the slip I got seemed boring, ho-hum. Since there were a few slips left over, I exchanged mine for a different one. Big mistake, since it was obviously meant for some other woman. It read simply: "I am frequently wrong."

First let me say that I've never heard that one. Not once. And second, how come the same thing always happens to me at Chinese restaurants? The fortune inside my cookie is always clearly intended for another person at the table. When it was my turn to share in that meeting, I didn't appreciate the way everyone laughed when I read my slip. It was almost like they thought it was perfect for me.

Thankfully, my husband can attest to the fact that I am frequently *right*. In fact, he's learned over the years not to second-guess me when I'm certain of a fact, because he hates being embarrassed when he's proved wrong.

But it was a mistake to tell Dave about what happened at the meeting. I even showed him my little strip of paper. He pretended to sympathize, but it was all an act, because the next morning I found the strip taped to the fridge.

I guess it's only natural that he would have some resentment about my ability to be right so often. Maybe I've asked him one too many times to, oh puleez, say my favorite three words to me. And they're not, "I love you." They're, "I . . . was . . . wrong."

During my drinking years, I thoughtfully provided Dave with tips on how to make a strong apology. I even boiled the key ideas down to three easy-to-remember As: Admit you were "wrong"; Affirm my hurt feelings; Ask my forgiveness.

Fortunately, I'm self-aware enough these days to recognize that I may not *always* be right. I'm sure I've been wrong. Somewhere in the past. Probably when I was still drinking.

But back to that slip of paper on the fridge. One day, just out of curiosity, I wondered, what would happen if I meditated on that phrase for a couple weeks? *I am frequently wrong. I am frequently wrong. I am frequently wrong.* I can recite those words in my head just fine. But why do I choke on them as they come out of my mouth? "I was wwwaah. I was wrrrrooo." It's just so hard to say!

Somewhere along the way, I think I learned that being wrong or mistaken is the same thing as being *weak*. Or *less*. Or *bad*.

But what if I did get totally comfortable with the idea of being wrong, even frequently wrong? How would it change me? Aside from the fact that Dave wouldn't recognize me, humility might look good on me.

Maybe you've heard the trick question: Do you want to be right, or do you want to be happy? I'd rather be both. But today, maybe, I'm going to choose to be happy. Just don't tell Dave.

An Offer
I Could Refuse

Once, a minister friend of mine offered me a permanent way out of my alcoholism. Blue eyes twinkling with sincerity, he said, "Heather, if you ever want to be finished with this thing, and never have to go to those meetings again—let me know. I'd be happy to pray with you. God wants to deliver you from this alcohol thing once and for all."

I smiled and nodded. It was a kind offer—but one I knew I'd never accept.

What my friend didn't understand was that I'm no longer *in bondage* to alcoholism; I'm liberated to rely completely on God to keep me sober. I don't *have* to go to these meetings, I *get* to. I'm not embarrassed to be a recovering drunk, I'm grateful.

Does it always feel good? No. In fact, some days, I wake up a little bit desperate. On many days, I have to learn all over again how to sit with an inner emptiness that I'd rather stuff with something more tangible than God's Spirit. Every morning, I have to let go of the control I think I want in order to receive the help I need.

Maybe for me, being alcoholic is like Paul having that thorn in his side. He tells us in 2 Corinthians 12 that he asked God to remove it three times. I asked God at least three *hundred* times to remove my addiction.

But God's response to Paul (and me, too) was not to remove it, reduce it, or zap it with a cure. Instead, God told Paul, "My grace is enough for you. My power is made perfect in weakness." In other words, *It's better for you to live with this thing.*

I've found this to be true. It is good to live in an ongoing posture of weakness that makes me have to rely on God's strength. It is good to be pricked by pain whenever I feel the inclination to try to run my own life again.

Henri Nouwen once wrote, "All addictions make us slaves, but each time we confess openly our dependencies and express our trust that God can truly set us free, the source of our suffering becomes the source of our hope."

Still, I understand where my friend was coming from. For the longest time, I too imagined that my alcoholism was nothing more or less than the absolute enemy. I was convinced that God and it were two opposing forces, good against evil. I often blamed it for all but shipwrecking my faith.

But now I know better. The truth is that I was spiritually waylaid long before I ever started drinking. My alcoholism was neither proof of my failure to love God, nor proof of God's failure to love me. It was a gift God saw way ahead before I ever got lost, to help guide me home.

Am I Sinning
or Am I Sick?

Disagreement over whether addiction is sin or sickness, choice or disease is common, especially in churches. But what is it about this sin-versus-sickness issue that gets people on both sides so heated? And why do labels matter anyway?

In treatment, I heard a saying that illustrates the difference between the two views: "We're not bad people getting good (sin paradigm), we're sick people getting well (sickness paradigm)."

When I was drinking I would have argued hard for the sin angle. The Bible says, "Do not be drunk with wine, but be filled with the Holy Spirit." Clearly—I thought—alcoholism is just the sin of drunkenness repeated over and over again.

With "do not be drunk" as my standard, I aimed not to drink to excess. When I did, I begged God for forgiveness. And then I asked God to help me not do it again. As the cycle of over-drinking, repentance, trying harder, and over-drinking again became a pattern, I often despaired.

Still, reminding myself that no temptation was too great for me with God's help, I kept on trying. I didn't consider physiological factors or genetic predisposition. I didn't understand that my personal response to alcohol—I got thirstier the more I drank—was abnormal.

Meanwhile, "do not get drunk" actually became a convenient escape clause. As my tolerance to alcohol steadily increased, I could drink an astonishing amount of alcohol without falling down, slurring my words, or otherwise seeming to appear drunk.

To meet the growing demand, I began to hide extra alcohol in my closet, telling myself it was Dave's fault. He just didn't get how much

I could drink without getting drunk. I preferred not to be judged by the glass.

It wasn't until I couldn't go a single day without drinking that I knew I was an alcoholic—whatever that was. At that point, I gave up repenting and instead began to beg God to deliver me from my obvious bondage.

I believe that God can and does instantaneously deliver people that way. *Whamo! You're free at last.* That person is likely to say, "I was delivered from alcoholism at the foot of the cross."

How desperately I wanted that to be me! Especially since my shame at being a Christian drunk made the idea of getting outside help unthinkable.

One morning in March of 2007, I woke up as usual—meaning that I couldn't remember the events of the previous evening. My eyes were swollen half-shut, like I'd been crying. I was terrified that I'd gotten into another dumb, "drunk Heather" fight with Dave the night before.

Exhausted, sick at heart, and overcome by despair, I found myself on my knees by my bed, sobbing. I don't remember what I prayed, or if it even involved words. I know I wailed incoherently—as if one of my children had died. I begged God for help in a way that made all my past attempts at surrender seem half-hearted by comparison.

Eventually, I quit crying and got up off of my knees. I felt strangely calm. I walked the dog. I drank my coffee. I knew that something big had happened. I was pretty sure that God had finally, miraculously delivered me.

But later that same afternoon, as I downed several glasses of Chardonnay, I was devastated. Clearly, I had not been given freedom from my awful obsession.

By the time Dave got home that evening, I understood what I'd been given instead though. I'd been given the ability to get over my pride, confess the truth to him, and ask for help.

Which in retrospect *was* a miracle.

Two weeks later, I went into treatment.

That's when I encountered the sickness paradigm first-hand. I was in a class led by a rehab counselor. The minute he called alcoholism a disease, my hand shot up.

"I'm sorry," I said, "but I always heard that calling alcoholism a *disease* was just an excuse. How can you call something a disease if it could have been avoided had you not participated in a certain behavior?"

Whew! I thought. *I'm so articulate!* I couldn't wait to hear this guy fumble for a response . . .

When Labels Mean Life and Death

So, I left off with my hand in the air, challenging an addiction counselor in treatment who dared to call alcoholism a "disease."

I thought my objection was righteous and clever.

But this guy had met my kind before, and he didn't blink. Instead, he calmly explained that alcoholism, like lung cancer caused by cigarettes or diabetes brought on by obesity, is a legitimate disease, even if it arises from an avoidable indulgence.

"And like other diseases," he added, "alcoholism is progressive. It gets worse over time, never better. Left untreated, it often results in death."

For the moment, I didn't have a comeback.

Later, as I brooded over his answer, I had to admit that treating my alcoholism purely as a sin problem hadn't worked. Here I was, after all.

Imagine my confusion when later this same counselor also described addiction as a spiritual malady that requires a spiritual solution.

Make up your mind, wouldya!

Today, I don't have that reaction. Instead of seeing addiction as a matter of sin *or* sickness, I think it involves *both*. We are sinners. *And* we are sick. When we battle compulsions and obsessions, we make choices that are fair to call sin. That is, we make choices that offend God and hurt us and others. But when these behaviors progress to the point of addiction, things get more complicated. Now we're dealing with a condition that includes very real physical, psychological, *and* spiritual components.

Personally, I take comfort in the fact that Jesus used the language of both sin and sickness to describe the reason he came: "Healthy people don't need a doctor—sick people do. I have come to call not those who think they are righteous, but those who know they are sinners." (Mark 2:17, NLT).

I introduced the question, do labels even matter?

Here are my thoughts about that: Honestly, I think a label can mean life or death. Because how we define a problem largely determines how or if we reach for a solution. If I have a disease, then it is treatable. But a label which is misapplied or used to shame an alcoholic into hiding, or to lead an addict to believe God has given up on him—that label could in effect kill. Couldn't it?

This is part of why I write Sober Boots. For more than a decade, that one-size-fits-all label—sin—actually kept me from reaching for the kind of help I needed.

It's easy when arguing ideas to forget that addiction destroys lives. It breaks hearts. It robs people of their dignity and hope. It keeps people from understanding how precious they are to God.

It takes our children.

During the years of my private drinking hell, I wish someone had sat me down and given me the good news: "You're *not* a uniquely horrible person, Heather. You're mentally, spiritually, and physically sick . . . and there *is* a solution."

How else but sick in body, mind, and spirit could you describe a mother who drinks so much she can't recall anything her kids told her the night before? Who, if she hasn't had enough alcohol, can't get her contacts in her eyes because her hands shake too much? Who, though she imagines she would die for her husband and children, can't quit drinking for them?

Today, I know I'm an ordinary person with a physical and mental predisposition that will never go away but that no longer defines my life.

And today I know I'm a sinner saved by grace—not just once so I can get into heaven, but every day so I can live sober, happy, and free.

We should all be so blessed.

When "Sin"
is a 5-Letter Word

One of the biggest gripes some Christians have about recovery programs which operate outside of church is that they don't use the word "sin" enough, or at all. I think the worry is that people who need God most won't know they're sinners and reach for the forgiveness Jesus bought for us on the cross.

I won't try to defend any particular program of recovery. But I do know people who came to know God through such communities who would have rejected a message that emphasized sin. Not because they don't think they sin, but mostly because they know they do.

Let me explain. The original meaning of the word "sin" is to fall short of an ideal or to "miss the mark." That's all of us. Every day. But these days, we're more likely to equate sin with evil and immorality. We imbue the word with a dark and loathsome intent. The result is that for many folks there's little or no space between a realization of *sin* and an experience of *shame*. And I'm guessing that this might be part of why many recovery programs avoid the word, since shame is so counterproductive for most people. It doesn't make an addict reach for God so much as run from him.

No wonder shame is our enemy's favorite counterfeit for true remorse. Healthy guilt or conviction about sin leads to repentance that carries with it the hope of forgiveness. But shame usually leads only to secrecy and lies. Shame screams at us that God is in the garden, so we better hide.

One of my favorite stories in the New Testament is only two sentences long. When Jesus is arrested and the disciples flee, we're told "A young man, wearing nothing but a linen garment, was following Jesus. When they seized him, he fled naked, leaving his garment behind."

(Mark 14:52, 53) This brief flash of bare buns has always struck me as funny. I imagine this guy's mother exclaiming, "But son! Why weren't you wearing a loincloth?"

The scene also takes me back to Adam and Eve in the garden: It reminds me how much of our faith journey is about trying to find our way back to "naked and not ashamed." It reminds me that Jesus came to free us, not only from the consequences of original sin, but from original shame, too.

It reminds me that God asks us to take radical risks to return home clothed, not in leaves or tunics, but in Christ alone. In recovery, we often remind one another that hurt people hurt people. In a similar sense, I think scared people scare people. And ashamed people shame people.

For that reason, I don't think a message about God should always lead with sin. What if instead, we lead with *love*? What if we focus less on the ugly thing Jesus came to defeat and more on what he won? *Forgiveness. Freedom. Relationship.* A chance to hear God coming near and to cry out with relief, rather than shame, "Here I am, Lord. Save me!"

Waking Up
Beloved

I wrote about how the word "sin" often evokes shame, especially in a recovery context. But shame is a human problem, and long-time Christians are in no ways immune.

I was a Christian for more than a decade before I became a slave to alcohol and shame. For me, shame came first.

After accepting Christ in my late teens, I was and anxious to spread the good news. But after the hallelujahs passed, I learned much more was required of me. I got busy with spiritual disciplines and a long list of dos and don'ts.

Meanwhile, I learned in church that when a person is born again, our "old man," the sin nature, dies and we become a new person: "Therefore, if anyone is in Christ, the new creation has come," writes Paul. "The old has gone, the new is here!" (2 Corinthians 5:17)

But I didn't feel new for very long. In fact, my capacity for sin seemed just as great as before I became a Christian. And the harder I tried to become more holy, the more guilty and burdened I felt. I decided that my "old man" had faked his death or my new self had gotten mangled in the spiritual birth canal. Either way, I was a failure and a fraud. Enter shame.

In shame's shadow, I grew disillusioned. Instead of hearing, "God loved me so much that he sent his son to die for me," I heard, "God hated me so much that he had to kill his own son just so he could stand to look at me."

The depths of my spiritual crisis came clear to me one night when I realized that I didn't share my faith with others because I wouldn't wish what I had on anyone. How sad is that?

I can't say what happened next—a lot of drinking—was the direct result of my spiritual discontent. But I do think a shame-based faith was fertile soil for the seeds of addiction.

Fortunately, I believe something different today. I think my "old man"—my ego-based, carnal self—will never die in the literal sense I once imagined that Paul was promising. Otherwise, why would New Testament writers so often remind us to walk, "according to the Spirit, not the flesh?"

After I got into recovery, I came to understand that Christ didn't die to eliminate my sin nature, *but to forgive me for having one.* As long as I'm alive, my "old man" will never die, reform, or even go on vacation. Ugly will always be ugly, even when I try to dress it up in JCrew.

This small shift in how I think is slowly reshaping my spiritual life. I still fight, flee, and resist sin, but I don't waste precious energy trying to conquer it beyond the present moment. I'm no longer shocked when sin hounds me, or when I wake up with a voice in my head that declares me queen of all I see. I just smile at my old self, then get on my knees.

I think it's natural that the more we know of God's goodness and holiness, the more we become aware of the actual depths of our depravity. But if we wake up to our sin without *also* waking up to our belovedness, we wake up in a nightmare.

These days, I try to focus most of my spiritual energies on nurturing and calling forward that "new creation" self. The self which is made in God's image, can't be tainted or diminished by sin, and is deeply rooted in God—or, as Paul put it, "Christ in you, the hope of glory."

I like to think of this self as my *real* self, my beloved self. This me is always saying yes to God and never doubts that God is smitten with her. Best of all, her face is never covered with shame.

Meanwhile, I've noticed that people who believe that the goodness of God actually dwells within them are more likely to see and serve love in others. I've noticed that people who know that they are *not* their sin are less likely to live in shame and more likely to fall with great relief into God's arms.

Today, that's me. And I wish what I have on everyone.

A Pig Story
for Grown-ups

In one of the gospel's stranger stories, Jesus meets a man who is possessed by a host of demons. We don't know the man's name, but we do know the demons'. Their name is Legion, and the man they torment lives alone among the tombs in pig country (Mark 5:1-18).

How did he get there? I'm guessing that for too many years he had been an impossible case. An embarrassment to his family. A menace to society. "And no one could bind him any more, not even with a chain," Mark tells us.

Enter Jesus. When he approaches, the demons correctly guess that they're about to be evicted. Like children trying to pick their punishment, they call out, "Hey, Jesus! How about instead of casting us out of the country, you send us into that yonder herd of pigs?"

Be careful what you ask God for. After Jesus grants their wish, the entire herd races off a cliff into a nearby lake where they drown.

I always used to imagine this scene with a couple dozen pigs, but I recently noticed the real number is *two thousand*. What did that stampede *sound* like? What did that lake *look* like? Did the town-folk have visions of free Jimmy Deans? (Wait a minute, Jewish people don't eat pork. So what were they doing with so many pigs?). All great questions, if you ask me.

But I think what Mark wants us to focus on here is the tormented man's transformation. A short time ago, this guy was a total maniac. Completely out of control: "Night and day among the tombs and in the hills he would cry out and cut himself with stones." Now he sits calmly before Jesus—sane, grateful, and restored.

And what does Jesus ask in return? He tells the man: "Go home to your family and tell them how much the Lord has done for you, and how he has had mercy on you."

The man gladly obeys, "and many in that town came to believe."

Given the cinematic setting, it's easy to miss that this is also a story about me. I too was once hopelessly tormented by compulsions I couldn't seem to escape. In recovery, we call it the "insanity" of alcoholism.

Day after day, I dashed myself against the rocks of my addiction. People who wanted to help me thought twice for good reason. I wasn't safe. And yet, here I sit before you today—sane (well, mostly), grateful, and sober. Now, numerous times a week, I tell my story in rooms filled with other recovering maniacs. They're people who used to live under bridges, or drive their children to school drunk, or shoot deadly drugs into their veins.

I tell them how it used to be, how God had mercy on me, and what it's like today. I listen to their stories in turn. And I come to believe all over again.

I wonder, do you have a deliverance story too? Maybe somewhere along the way you hurt yourself or others and you couldn't change or stop. You ended up isolated and alone. You lived in shame and wallowed in secret misery. And then God came. A pig may not have drowned in the making of your miracle. But God met you among the tombs. And he had mercy on you and he rescued you. Now you have a story to tell.

P.S. I got on the internet and checked. Lo and behold, pigs can swim—just not when they're demon-possessed.

The Hunger Games, Hope, and Hitting Bottom

I t wasn't my plan, but I've seen the *The Hunger Games* twice now. As often happens for me, one particular line of dialogue in the movie stood out.

The evil President Snow, concerned that the heroine's courage will inspire a rebellion among his oppressed subjects, warns his underling, "A little hope is effective, but a lot of hope is dangerous."

The first part of this statement is especially true for addicts. A little hope *is* effective to keep a person oppressed by addiction from acting to escape. As long as an addict has the slightest hope that he can continue to manage his life without having to surrender his obsession, he won't.

This explains why in recovery we say the more hopeless an active drunk is, the better. Hopelessness is synonymous with "hitting bottom." *Bottom* is that place of misery so deep that an addict is finally more desperate to find a way out of his addiction than he is to feed it.

This truth has important implications for the family and friends of any addict. Especially in the case of alcohol and drugs, "helping" an addict to manage the fallout of his choices can keep his hope alive just long enough to spell his death.

Especially if you're a parent, this is a hard message to hear. Rushing in to rescue our kids, keeping hope afloat for them, is what we do best. Plus, since many addicts *don't* hit bottom until they're six feet under, we know that letting go doesn't guarantee anything, either. So what should parents, friends, or spouses of addicted loved ones do?

Speaking from experience, I think you should do what I failed to when my own son was losing his life to drugs and alcohol. Seek help for *yourself* in a community such as, Alanon, Codependants Anonymous, or Celebrate Recovery.

Loving an addict isn't for sissies *or* the self-reliant. A community of caring people who share similar heartaches can offer priceless comfort and support. Plus, you'll learn the powerful meaning behind the saying: "You didn't cause it, you can't control it, and you can't cure it." I learned first-hand that addiction tends to run in families. But the good news is that recovery runs in families, too. On numerous occasions I've watched it spread like a beautiful contagion through families and beyond.

And here's more good news. The second piece of President Snow's observation is also true. While a little hope is effective to keep a person in bondage, "a *lot* of hope is dangerous" to whatever keeps them bound—in this case, the power of addiction itself.

Paradoxically, one of the first things many addicts experience when they're new in recovery is a *lot* of hope. I'll never forget how it felt to look around in a meeting and realize these people shared my seemingly un-fixable problem—yet they'd found a way out. And they looked happy!

In that same bit of dialogue, President Snow also says: "Hope is the only thing stronger than fear." Well, I think he's right again. Hope *has* to be more powerful than fear because so many of us fear hope itself. Let's face it. Few things in life hurt worse than hope that is dashed or disappointed. So why should we even dare to hope for those we love who are captives to an addiction?

The Psalms are filled with statements like, "Happy are those trust in God," and "He who hopes in the Lord will not be disappointed." I used to think that meant people who hope in God get the outcome they want, so *of course* they're happy. But now I read these passages differently. I think they're saying that we're happy *as* we trust God, because hope sustains us, brings us peace, and helps us relax into the knowledge that God is good, *no matter what*. What will be will be. But for you and me, right now, hope can be its own reward.

P.S. An important piece that relates to this one and could sound contradictory is "For the Loved Ones" on page 200xx. What I mean by the importance of hopeless here is about an addict becoming hopeless *about his ability to manage or conquer his addiction on his own.* In reality, without hope, most addicts won't want their lives enough to want to face them sober.

10 Ways NOT to Help

've never thought of myself as a particularly caring or giving person. I used to worry that at my funeral no one would have nice things to say about me—you know, things like, "Heather would give you the shirt off her back." In the old days, if I gave you the shirt off my back, I was probably drunk, and later might accuse you of stealing it.

In sobriety, I've been learning a better way. Helping others is part of what keeps me healthy and happy. But a lot of my friends are addicts and alcoholics—people like me who are famously hard to help. And lately, it's been a heart-breaking venture.

One thing I am learning is that helping anyone is a lot like dancing. It takes two—one to give help and one to receive. So when helping someone starts to feel super hard, I'm probably part of the problem.

Here are some of my most recent mistakes:

1. **I offer to do things I later resent.** I say yes to a favor because I want to be generous and I want you to think I'm nice. But later, when it costs me time and energy, I grumble and complain to myself, or even to Dave. That's just not fair or right.

2. **I want to save the day.** And what better way to do that than to succeed in helping someone where others have failed? Two things: If the person does well, I'll take credit. If they don't, I'll take blame. Both miss the point. The idea isn't to be a hero or make a person think *you* are the answer. What a set up!

3. **I act out of short-sighted fear.** Sometimes I "help" because I am afraid to let people experience the consequences of their actions. I don't trust the process, in other words. I do what makes me—and maybe the person—feel better right now.

4. **I over-invest.** When you truly love a person and want to help them, it's easy to put more into solving their problems than they are. Next thing you know, they're less motivated than before because *you* feel all the urgency. Plus, you could be helping other people who don't just need help but *want* it.

5. **I attach expectations.** I never mean to do this, but I attach strings that I don't see until they start to strangle *me*. I expect gratitude; I expect the person to take all my advice; I expect them to make me look good . . . Pretty soon I'm swearing under my breath.

6. **I get caught up in drama.** When you're helping someone with bigger problems than yours, drama can act like a drug—it's distracting, energizing, and gives you purpose. Pretty soon, you've got your nose way too deep in someone else's business.

7. **I forget that God loves people.** It's easy to think that God is not paying attention to the person who seems to be flailing. We imagine that God can show up for them *only* through us. But God is at work and pursuing this person just as hard as he lovingly pursues me.

8. **I deny what's at stake.** When I get deeply invested with a person's welfare, I forget to count the cost, to remember that the outcome might be awful. Knowing the risks doesn't remove them, but it makes me feel more calm when I remember that I can't control outcomes.

9. **I overstep my role.** I get into trouble when I forget to step back from a highly charged situation and ask, What is my role here? Having a legitimate role like "mom" or "sponsor" can make it even easier to lose sight of what's really your responsibility. It's important to ask, "Is there someone more suitable or qualified to address this person's need?"

10. **I ignore my safety.** People in trouble often end up in bad places and dangerous situations. It's easy for me to forget discretion and put myself at risk—which just isn't smart.

Do you recognize yourself in any of these? Can you think of some other common mistakes we make in our efforts to help?

Here's the balance, though. It's also possible to get so worried about boundaries that we miss the big picture. If someone's life is in imminent danger, or if a child or innocent will be hurt—you act. You barge in. You help. You don't say, "Well, gee. As your teacher (or peer or neighbor), that's not my job."

Sure, but is it your job as a human being?

I think of the parable Jesus told about the man left beaten by the side of the road. Fortunately, the good Samaritan who saved him hadn't read too many books on boundaries.

Above all, don't be too hard on yourself when you screw up. Better to fail trying to help someone than to walk on by.

I'm So Glad I Had You

When my youngest son Nathan was about four years old, he picked up a phrase from me. "I'm so glad I had you!" he'd say proudly, beaming up at me from under a tousle of white blond hair.

"No, Nathan," I'd tell him, laughing. "Remember, I had *you*!"

That happened—I had Nathan—27 years ago. Yesterday was his birthday.

Back in October, Nathan and his fiancé, Kelsey, came for a three-week visit. It seemed like a good time to ask Nathan to read the latest draft of my memoir. I printed it out, left it on his bed, and told him that if he got a chance, I'd love to hear his thoughts.

After a week, he still hadn't cracked a page. I reminded myself that Nathan had already seen an early partial draft. Obviously, he wasn't in a hurry to finish the story. But since he's one of my biggest supporters, I wondered why. Toward the end of the visit, I casually asked.

"I do want to read it—and I will," he said. "But actually, Mom, I have a lot of good memories from my childhood. I loved our family and I loved growing up in Sisters. So it makes me sad that you want go back and paint everything black because of your drinking."

His words startled me. On the one hand, it was wonderful to hear him say he'd had a happy childhood—my drinking issues hadn't ruined that for him. But he was also saying something else, and I needed to hear it. His experience wasn't mine. And my experience wasn't his.

Given that I hid a great deal of my excess drinking from my family, it makes sense that Nathan feels some disconnect from my story. I recall things like missing one of his touchdown receptions because I was guzzling beers in a bathroom stall. But Nathan recalls that his mom was cheering him on from the sidelines.

No wonder he wants to protect his good memories from my bad ones.

In thinking about what he said, I'm reminded of how easy it is for me to imagine the past in black and white when it's really a kaleidoscope of colors. How tempting it is to let one dark truth paint the whole canvas of my story.

Nathan helped me to reclaim the good times our family experienced over the years. How we camped, took hikes, and had long wonderful evenings in the homes of friends. I was reminded of how the house was always packed with teenage boys, the smell of sweaty socks, guitars lying everywhere, and music filling the air.

Why would I want to forget any of that? It's the most important part of my story, really—that gleaming thread of redemption that runs through it. The parts where God watched over my kids and brought them good when I couldn't. The parts where God loved me even as I drank in a bathroom stall.

Thank you, Nathan, for having me for a mom.

I'm so glad I had you!

It's Not the Coffee

Do you ever wonder why people in recovery are always dashing off to meetings?

Is the coffee really that good? (Umm ... only if you bring your own).

Are other alcoholics really that entertaining? (Sometimes, yes).

At some point, haven't you learned all you need to know? (Absolutely not!).

Sunday, Dave and I flew home from a conference we'd been attending in Michigan. Yesterday, I wasted the whole day wrestling with a blog post about ego—and lost.

Last night, when I told Dave I'd had a really rough day, he suggested we go sit outside at a favorite restaurant—so *he* could have a martini.

No, he wasn't being mean. He knew I would laugh. These days, Dave knows he can have a drink in front of me and I will hardly notice or care. Alcohol is no longer my main problem. My main problem is *me*.

This morning I realized that maybe the problem with me today—and yesterday—is that I haven't been to a single meeting for a week. And I usually go to four. Could this be why I've felt so out of sorts lately? *Duh!*

Later today, I will walk around the corner to a nearby church. We'll light candles, place them on the floor in the middle of our circle of chairs. Then we'll sit in quiet meditation for ten minutes before we begin to share.

My soul will settle back into its sockets.

I feel a wave of relief just writing those words. So it seems like a good morning to tell you five reasons I still go to so many meetings and hope I always will.

1. **This is my community.** Dave and I attend a church in town that never fails to feed me spiritually. And yet, it's in the intimate atmosphere of my meetings that I feel most known, recognized, and "part of."
2. **This is my medicine.** We're never *cured* of alcoholism, but we do have a *solution*—one drunk talking to another. Just as doctors can't explain how certain drugs treat certain conditions, the fact that regular meetings keep an alcoholic well is a proven fact—part mystery and part miracle.
3. **This is my reminder.** Since most of us are great forgetters, meetings help us recall the basic spiritual principles and tools we have at our disposal. It's a lot like church—we don't always hear something new, but we often hear what we need to hear today.
4. **This is my ministry.** I've never aspired to ministry and don't love the word. But when you get right down to it, this is what happens in the rooms of recovery. People who never felt of much use to anyone find new purpose in serving and helping others.
5. **This is my chance to ask for help.** I am still working on this. I tend to show up looking for ways to give—partly because I want to help, partly because it helps me feel good. But just as you can only keep what you give away—you can only give away what you're also willing to receive. One of the most life-changing things I've ever uttered in a meeting was the simple admission, "I think I need your help."

If you're not an alcoholic in recovery, right about now I bet you wish you were. It's so sad that everyone doesn't get to be a drunk! But I'll tell ya what. If you're ever in my area, I'll take you to an open meeting. It will be fun. Really. And I promise—we'll go *out* for coffee.

Unless You Fall

Dave and I see a lot of small, independent movies at an old-fashioned theater downtown. Afterward, we go straight next door for ice cream and talk about the film, let it settle in our souls.

Some movies linger for days or weeks, while others you forget right away. Sometimes, a single moment or scene comes back to you later out of the blue because it has something to do with your life at the moment—even if you're not sure what.

That happened to me this morning. As Dave and I walked our dog, I noticed the weather was slightly off; they were predicting an April thunderstorm. Something in the air reminded me of a brilliant little film we saw about six months ago called, *Another Earth*.

After Dave left for work, I came upstairs to write, and a scene from that movie rose to mind and hovered there. In it, the main female character is talking to a man tortured by a tragic loss; she begins to gently knock on the table while she tells him a story.

It's about a Russian cosmonaut. He's the first ever to orbit the earth from space. He's up there alone; his window portal is small; he's lost in wonder as he gazes at his planet home.

But then he hears a knocking sound. It is rhythmic, but constant. Knock . . . knock . . . knock. . . . After a while, he becomes desperate to make the noise stop. He tears apart the control panel, trying to find the source of the sound.

But he can't. He still has twenty-five days left in space, and he knows he'll never make it. Locked up in this capsule with the knocking sound, he's certain he will go insane.

Unless.

Unless is a hopeful word here.

Unless he can find a way to fall in love with this exact sound. Unless it becomes to him the most beautiful noise in the world.

The story ends with the cosmonaut floating through space in a symphony.

And it dawns on me what this scene has to do with me. Earlier this morning, before I walked with Dave, I sat in my chair and shut my eyes. I smelled the hot flame of my candle. I felt the weight of a favorite book in my lap. I heard a dove cooing outside the window behind my head.

And it was not enough.

Life as God gives it—reality—falls short. Even when it is generous and good, as my life has been lately. Something is flat that should be round; something is empty that demands to be full; and you can't say what is missing or why.

Some days, ordinary life is as relentless as that knocking sound.

Unless, God whispers to me. *Unless you fall in love with it . . .*

I think about the cosmonaut, the earth in his window, the music in his head. Can I be that brave today?

I think about thunder in April in Colorado, the way a film can pierce your soul, the way sometimes grace makes up for what life lacks.

And I let myself fall . . .

I still hear the knocking sound; but it is my own heart beating with love for this world.

Once Upon
a Sneaky Prayer

Once upon a time I met a little prayer I hated on sight. Maybe that was part of the problem—I didn't *hear* it so much as *see* it everywhere: Cross-stitched on pillows, emblazoned on posters, or decoupaged onto wooden plaques from the '70s.

Clearly it was the cliché of all prayers, and not to be taken seriously by thinking people like myself. So when I discovered this silly prayer was a favorite among recovery folk, I was embarrassed: Really? That's the best you can do?

Of course, I'm talking about The Serenity Prayer:

God, grant me the serenity to accept the things I cannot change,
the courage to change the things I can,
and the wisdom to know the difference.

I didn't get it. What does this prayer have to do with *not* drinking?

For months, I prayed along in unison, but without enthusiasm. Until one day, I finally heard what the words were actually saying. What they were telling me was that I lived the prayer in reverse:

Trying to change people and situations I can't possibly control.
Failing to change what I can and should.
Neglecting to ask for wisdom before I charge ahead.

When I live this way, forcing my will against the flow of life, I lose any sense of inner peace or calm. In place of serenity, I reach for escape, distraction, or the kind of numbness I used to get from alcohol. *This* is what the prayer has to do with addiction.

Once I made this connection, I began to say this prayer with new intention. And today, I get it, why it's worked wonders for so many millions of people. It's not a silly prayer, at all—it's a sneaky prayer. Tucked within it is a powerful prescription for living in harmony with the world no matter what life brings.

Today, I often use this prayer to help me sort out how I should respond when I feel anxious, confused, or overwhelmed. On paper or in my head, I put troubling situations into columns:

Column 1. *Things I cannot change* because I have absolutely no control over them. My best response: Let it go. Give it to God. Don't waste any more time or energy on it.

Column 2. *Things I could and should change* but I lack the confidence or courage to act. My best response: Ask God for willingness. Determine the next right step. Choose to act.

Column 3. *Things I need wisdom to sort out* because they fall into neither column or both. My best response: Pause. Be slow to respond. Pray for discernment. Possibly seek counsel.

And then there's Column 4: *Things that are simply none of my business.* Okay, this isn't part of the prayer, but it seems like it should be!

These days, Dave and I often use these columns as a fun shorthand. For example, the other day, I'm whining about how I can't believe I haven't been to yoga for four months when Dave interjects, "Isn't that...Column 2?"

He's right, of course. It's a clear case of something that is up to me to change—and I could, if I wanted to, but . . .

Well, you get the idea.

Like I said, it's a sneaky little prayer.

But it could just change your life today.

Smack Dab
in the Center

A friend recently told me, "I keep praying under my breath, 'God, your will not mine,' but I don't think I really mean it."

Her honesty sparked a conversation about how we both come from Christian backgrounds where we got the wrong idea about God's will—in short, that it is probably gonna suck. Or hurt. Or be way too hard.

In my case, I also learned that the only thing harder than doing God's will is figuring out what it is. And woe to you if you miss it. Get one degree off track today and in a few years you'll find yourself deep in the boonies where God can't bless you.

This belief led to the kind of silliness wherein I ignored God's clear will regarding the big stuff—like love, honesty, and compassion—while I treated random twitches of the universe like spiritual Morse code meant to help me decipher God's will on important matters—like which car to buy.

But I've been learning a new approach. To my surprise, a lot of people in recovery talk a lot about doing God's will, not ours, but minus the hand-wringing, confusion and fear. Many of them operate on the radical assumption that God is good, wants our best, and if we just do the next right thing he puts in front of us, we'll be fine. Crazy stuff, huh?

Some time ago, Dave and I went for a hike near where we lived in Colorado. The trail followed a creek up a steep canyon. Mostly it did, anyway. Actually, the trail split, disappeared, reappeared, and crisscrossed the creek so often that it was impossible to tell if we were following the "right" trail. It also didn't really matter. The entire hike followed the creek. Follow the water and we'd be fine.

Later this week, I have a big decision to make regarding a project that's close to my heart. And it's got me wondering: What if God's will for me—or for any of us—is as wide and deep and roomy as that canyon? It would mean that regardless of which rock I step on, or which path I follow, if I stay near the creek, I'm still in the middle of God's will. It would also mean that to miss God's will, I'd have to leave the creek and start huffing it up the side of the canyon—and I couldn't accomplish that without noticing what I was doing.

I find this metaphor deeply comforting. It also matches up pretty well with what I believe about God today. I think he wants me to seek his will for me, but not because he's hiding it. I think he asks me to want what he wants—not so I can suffer, but so others and I won't.

So this week, I'm praying for guidance. And yes I'm telling God, "Your will not mine," and meaning it. But I also feel like I'm rambling through a wide-open space with God's Spirit running through it, and there's no place I'd rather be. And if I spot an appealing rock ahead— one that looks friendly, put there just for me, and steady enough to hold my dreams—I'm free to leap. Or not. Either way, how much you wanna bet I land smack dab in the center of God's will?

Eat Right Now

This morning, I'm thinking about what I can't accumulate. Not sobriety. Not holiness. Not courage.

It's so easy, given my desire to control the world and to feel secure, to think I can borrow from yesterday's store or fix tomorrow's problems today.

But the truth is so simple that I miss it: I can't stay sober on yesterday's recovery. I can't make tomorrow's surrender today. I can't conquer fear in advance of the need to be brave.

So this morning I'm thinking that all I have is today. *Give us this day our daily bread*... I can only eat right now. I can only get what God gives me in this moment. I can only be what I am right this second.

Out of the Mouths of Drunks

When I first took a chair in the rooms of recovery, I couldn't wait to impress all the down and out, spiritually lost people I met there with my vast store-house of Christian wisdom. Only a few weeks into my journey, I actually thought to myself, "I think I can help some of these poor folks."

In reality, I had a great deal to learn from them—more than I ever dreamed.

The following list is by no means exhaustive, but it reflects some of the most important truths I've gleaned from my fellow drunks—or as I like to think of them, beautifully broken people. Some are popular sayings you'd hear in any meeting. In other cases, I've added my own twist.

Ten Things I've Learned In the Rooms of Recovery

1. Expectations of others are premeditated resentments.

2. You can't keep what you have unless you give it away.

3. God can do for me what I can't do for myself—but first I have to give up trying.

4. In God's hands our broken past can become our greatest asset.

5. We don't need something to fill our emptiness, just the courage to leave it empty.

6. We can't feel comfortable in every situation, but we can get more comfortable with being uncomfortable.

7. A problem is something we can change but won't—or something we can't change, but won't accept.

8. Drama and crisis are usually optional.

9. Every problem has a spiritual solution.

10. What you think about me is none of my business.

Is Addiction Stronger Than Love?

My friend Becca looks like a model, lives in a beautiful home, and has an adoring husband and three young children. But she's also an alcoholic who struggles to stay sober. For the past ten months she's worked hard to recover from a series of devastating relapses that almost cost her everything—including her marriage and kids.

A few weeks ago, I attended a surprise party she threw for one of her children. It also felt like a celebration of Becca's return to health and happiness. She looked radiant. Her kids clung to her. Her husband beamed with obvious pride. Only days later, she relapsed again. Friday, she called me crying and asked for help.

I went to see her where she's staying—a skanky, drive-up motel, the kind where drugs are rampant and no one is actually on vacation. I hardly recognized her. She looked scary thin. Her eyes were flat and dead, her face blotchy. She couldn't sit up, kept falling sideways. Clothing and garbage were strewn everywhere. She denied being drunk or on drugs, but she could barely form the words, "I'm not lying." And there, on a nightstand by the bed—a mattress with no sheets—was a beautiful framed photo of her three kids.

The incongruity and irony made me want to scream, "How could you! Don't you love your kids? How could you do this to your husband again!" I drove home in tears, haunted by a question I've asked myself for years: *Is addiction stronger than love?*

Sure seems like it. I couldn't quit drinking to save my son from his own alcoholism. I couldn't quit drinking for my husband, either. If he'd given me an ultimatum—"I love you, babe, but it's me or alcohol"—I might have chosen alcohol.

But this weekend, after seeing Becca, I found myself thinking differently. I decided that addiction isn't really stronger than love *because love has nothing to do with it.* Today I am more convinced than ever that addiction is a mental illness. What else but *insanity* can turn caring mothers into uncaring monsters, loyal spouses into liars and cheaters, promising sons and daughters into criminals and whores?

I'm reminded of one of the best zombie movies ever made, "28 Days Later." It's often confused with the Sandra Bullock movie about an addict going through rehab, "28 Days." But in a way, both films depict the same horrific scenario—what happens when good people morph into something less than human. Which is part of what makes zombies so scary. Unlike monsters or aliens, these people still look like your loved ones or neighbors, except they're not anymore.

The same can be said of an addict. The Becca I saw in the motel on Friday was not the Becca I know and love. She was like the living dead, incapable of choosing love. And where does that leave her husband? Tonight he's probably still wondering, "Why doesn't she love me enough to quit?" He's putting their small children to bed alone. They're asking, "Daddy, where's Mommy?" And he has no answer. The mommy they love has disappeared.

In all of this, hope is so hard to find, but it's there if you look. Addiction might seem stronger than love, but God is stronger than addiction. Because this is true, some addicts do come back from the dead. I did.

I'm writing this piece as a zombie in full remission. Becca just might come back, too.

Yes to Nuthin

This morning, I looked forward to writing something not related to recovery or controversy. I asked God for something light, perhaps even funny. Yet poignant. You know, something to entertain and help my readers.

I put in my order, I'm telling you.

And I got nuthin.

It's a big fear with regard to writing. And it happens to me often in real life, too. Just when I really want to say something profound, I reach for impressive, shiny words and they turn to ashes in my mouth.

In this morning's daily reading was the familiar story of the rich young man who comes to Jesus with a big question: "What can I do to inherit eternal life?"

When Jesus tells him to keep the commandments, he responds with a tinge of pride. "I already got those down. Actually, I've had 'em licked since I was a kid. So what else ya got?"

What comes next always stops me in my tracks. Mark's version tells us, "Jesus looked at him and loved him."

Wait. Jesus loves everyone. And yet, nowhere else are we told that Jesus loved someone on sight like this. And I always wish it was me Jesus was looking at this way.

But only for a second, since in his next breath Jesus goes and ruins everything. "One thing you still lack," he tells the young man. "Go sell all you have and give it to the poor and come follow me."

I always think, *C'mon, Jesus! Give the guy a break! How about he gives away half?*

I'm not worried about the guy's money or the poor, actually. I just want a happy ending. And I know what's coming next. It's one of the saddest sentences in the Bible.

"But because the young man was very rich, he went away sad."

For many years, I read this story as a cautionary tale about wealth and idolatry: Whatever you love more than God will keep you from the kingdom.

When I was still drinking, I knew that if you replaced this young man's stash of riches with my secret stash of wine, you'd get me—unable to give up my treasure. So I too went away sad. For twelve long years.

But now I see something more. Maybe Jesus knew this guy understood spirituality the same way he did money; that is, you can only get more by adding. Which would explain why he asks Jesus in effect, What more can I do? What would put me over the top?

I think I used to see my spiritual life that way too. I was on a mission to accumulate holiness and spiritual kudos. Since I didn't want to give up what I loved most (my wine), I hoped I could add some things instead. Make up the difference.

Trouble was, Jesus wasn't looking for addition. He was looking for subtraction. Like the rich young ruler, *what I really lacked was lack itself.* I couldn't see my own spiritual poverty, which, had I embraced, would have driven me to God, desperate for his grace.

Ironically—coming up empty—probably doesn't happen to me *enough.*

So this morning, I open my Bible and meet Jesus on the page and he asks me once again to make what author Brennan Manning calls "the great exchange": Everything I *think* I have for everything only God can give.

If you don't come to me empty, Jesus says, *all you'll have to offer is the self you are so full of.*

I hesitate for a moment. It doesn't feel like an entirely safe trade.

But then he looks at me, and I know he loves me.

And I say yes to nuthin.

Nothing But
a Burning Light

This time of year, I see dead moths. Everywhere. This morning, I carefully studied the corpses of two who died on my bathroom windowsill. I couldn't believe how complicated their bodies, how detailed their tiny, delicate parts.

But why, and for what are their lives? All moths seem to do is bounce off windows, lampshades, and my head while I'm trying to read my book at night. Plus, they operate in a state of constant confusion:

Ooh! The light! I want to fly into the light!
Ouch! Ooh! The window!
I want to fly into the window! Bam!

As the death toll rises and small brown carcasses litter my house, I'm reminded that none of us will make it out of here alive.

Worse, today it feels to me like our human endeavors are as silly and pointless as these moths. We dash from one thing to the next, accomplishing little, slamming into the same obstacles over and over. And for what?

Oh, don't mind me. On Saturday, I will turn a new number, even though I don't want to. So it's probably just my birthday that has me thinking mothy thoughts.

Annie Dillard once described the demise of a moth in a beautiful essay. She was reading outside by candlelight when she saw one fly straight into her candle, get stuck in the wax, and burn. As she watched, the moth's body turned into a second wick, and for a while, her candle burned twice as bright.

If we are like moths, then God is our flame. We're drawn to his light for reasons we can barely name. But we feel afraid, too. Our God is a consuming fire. So we come close enough to warm ourselves, but not so close we'll singe our wings. We circle, flit about, get lost and confused.

But what if we were meant for more? What if we were meant to fly straight into the flame? What if we were meant to go all in, to become consumed with what consumes God most—his love for this world?

Perhaps my problem today isn't the dead moths or even my birthday—but my fear that I'm too selfish to catch fire. And maybe what I want most is to lose my life in God's until I'm—in the words of Bruce Cockburn—I'm nothing but a burning light.

The Next Knock
at My Door

You've probably heard people say your feelings can't kill you. They're just feelings, after all. But I'm here to tell you they can.

Recently, I sat at my dining room table with a dear friend who is a successful, career-oriented woman. She's also dangerously overweight. "How can such a smart person not be able to figure this out?" she asked me, tears streaming.

My friend admits she uses food to numb unwanted feelings of guilt, sadness, and anger. "Ice cream got me through my divorce," she says.

Ice cream, cocaine, sex, booze—I completely get it.

The biggest problem with addictions is that they *work*. For a while, whatever it was you didn't want to feel, you feel less or not at all. Sooner than you dreamed possible, you're hooked. What began as a handy escape escalates into a destructive addiction that could someday take your life.

When a person who has been numb for years finally seeks help, the return of emotions can come as quite a shock. In recovery, we sometimes say with a wink to newcomers, "Don't worry, you'll feel better soon." But what we mean is you'll feel *everything* better soon— including pain, resentment, anger, boredom, sadness, guilt…

No wonder learning how to feel our feelings is such an important part of recovery (and a good way to help prevent addictions, too).

I don't know about you, but when painful feelings knock at my door, I tend to respond in one of two ways. One is to fling the door open wide and let my feelings barge in, create chaos, stomp all over me—and eventually, everyone else, too.

The other response is to shove a piano in front of the door, suppressing what I don't want to feel in hopes it will go away. If it does, I usually find myself depressed. I think that's because when I refuse to feel sad, I lose the ability to feel happy, too.

Lately, I've been trying to practice a middle way, a more intentional approach. It goes something like this: When negative feelings knock, I open the door and stick my head out. "Ah, I see you there," I say. "I feel you."

Sometimes, I invite them to stay for a while. I sit down in my favorite chair. I become very still. I might light a candle. I notice what is happening in my body and heart. I give my feelings my full attention. I try not to judge them as "good" or "bad," "wrong" or "right."

Instead, I ask, "Why is guilt, anger, or pain visiting me today? What does it want to teach me?" If I feel a need to express strong emotions, I do—even if it means a private mini-tantrum.

And guess what happens next? My feelings don't hurt nearly as much as I feared they would. You may have heard it said, what you resist—persists. That's definitely true with feelings—and so is its opposite. As I surrender to hurtful or scary emotions, the monster loses some of its teeth.

I can *respond* instead of just *react*.

I don't have to eat or drink or do anything to escape or get numb.

I get to experience every second of my awful, wonderful life in all its aching glory.

And who knows? The next knock at my door might be joy.

Does God Answer Slurred Prayers?

B ecause I was a Christian long before I became an alcoholic, a part of me always understood that God was my only hope. Some nights, I'd get drunk and beg God to do a miracle and make me stop. In the morning, sick with shame and regret, I'd remind myself: *God doesn't answer slurred prayers, Heather.*

But is that really true? What if God not only hears those prayers, he's willing to help drunks get sober—even if they don't pray in Jesus name, or even if they use a recovery program that isn't exclusively Christian?

I'm a little embarrassed to admit that when I first got into recovery, it shocked me to see God so clearly at work in the lives of people who didn't call him by the "right" name or necessarily identify themselves as Christians.

The longer I attended meetings among such folks, the more I saw that not only was God helping them to recover, in many cases, they depended on him in a more *actual* way than I ever had—like a crippled person leans on and trusts a cane.

I noticed something else, too. No matter what people called their "higher power," it always sounded a lot like the God of the Bible—good, loving, just, and forgiving. What did it all mean?

Today, I think it means that left to their own devices, people seem naturally drawn to an idea of God inscribed on their hearts by their Creator. I think it means that God can and does draw people to himself without the help of expert Christians, church, or the Bible. I think it means that God's kindness is so great and his love so far-reaching that he rushes to the aid of any who cry out to him for help.

The Jaws of Distress

'm pretty sure some of you woke up this morning with a terrible hangover, bloated from a food-binge, or mortified about who you slept with last night. I know this because you write to me and say, "You are me! I am you!" And then you describe just how horribly caught you feel. How desperately you want to quit the eating or drinking or sleeping around, but can't seem to.

I've exchanged emails with a woman recently who described how she is hoping to conquer her alcoholism by practicing a new level of honesty. "Karen" is confessing to people. She is asking her friends to pray for her. She is diving into a truth-telling way of life that she hopes can save her. And maybe it will. I hope it will. A willingness to be rigorously honest is one of the cornerstones of recovery, because it sets us free from the lies of shame that keep us isolated and stuck.

But for most of us, honesty is not enough. A majority of addicts need the tools, fellowship, and support of a recovery community.

One question Karen asked me was, "What verses did you use?" *To help you stop drinking,* she meant. I told her that while I was drinking I had used Bible verses mostly to beat myself up. To prove to myself that if I only loved God more, repented more fully, or was a better person or Christian, I could quit.

I never found that magic verse, which if understood and applied rightly, could break my chains of addiction once and for all. One recent morning, though, I came across this line in Job: "He is wooing you from the jaws of distress to a spacious place free from restriction." —Job 36:16.

Wait a minute, I thought. Why would God have to "woo" us from the "jaws of distress?" Why wouldn't we happily run to that spacious place of freedom?

Then I remembered how one of the most baffling aspects of addiction is that for a long time we resist our own rescue. It sounds crazy, but it's true.

I think it goes like this: Part of us wants deliverance. But another part of us is so deeply attached to our substance or activity that as long as it still brings us more pleasure than pain, we can't let go. We may holler for help, but we also hold on tight.

Maybe this explains why God so rarely arrives in a cloud of glory to liberate us with just the right verse or truth. More often, he uses our distress, gently wooing us through our misery toward surrender. At least, that's how it was for me.

Twelve Things That Kept Me Stuck

Sometimes, when I look back on the twelve years plus that I was active in my alcoholism, I wonder why I didn't reach for help sooner. What kept me stuck for so long?

Every addict's experience is unique, including what keeps us from seeking recovery. But we share in common much more than we don't. So I offer this stuck list from my life in the hopes it might help you or someone you love get unstuck sooner instead of later.

I stayed stuck because . . .

1. **I Believed Shame's Lie.** I was convinced that if I revealed the true extent of my drinking problem, a crushing avalanche of shame would bury me alive. But the opposite was true. I never suffered worse shame than I felt while hiding my secret, nor have I ever experienced greater relief than after it came out. *Secrets don't protect us from shame, they create it.*

2. **I Wanted a Third Way.** I hated living as an alcoholic. But neither did I want to live sober. I wanted the third way, one where I could be like other people and control my drinking. But for an alcoholic such a road is pure fantasy. He or she might stop drinking *but no alcoholic ever becomes a normal drinker.*

3. **I Was Terrified that "Help" Would Fail Me.** I had already seen that every time I repented and swore off drinking, I couldn't stay stopped. So what if I got help but *still* couldn't stop? That was such a scary prospect that it seemed safer not to try. Now I know better. *While there is no cure for*

alcoholism, there is a solution *for anyone who is willing to work hard.*

4. **I Needed the Scales of Misery to Tip.** I wasn't willing to even consider sobriety until my present misery was so great that it eclipsed the misery I imagined being sober would bring. *Now I know that the enduring joys of recovery far outshine the fleeting pleasures of addiction.*

5. **I Didn't Want to Change.** I knew if I got sober, Dave and others would expect more of me. I'd have to take responsibility for my life and behavior and relationships in a new way. It was easier to stay unhappy in the same, predictable ways. *Now I understand that recovery changes what you want. Before long, you welcome the opportunity to grow.*

6. **I Was Afraid of Wearing the Scarlet A.** Because I attached a shameful stigma to alcoholism, I dreaded having that label attached to me. I feared prejudice, disdain, loneliness, career repercussions. I mean, who wants to be friends with an alcoholic? Turns out, lots of people. *Now I welcome the chance to help change stereotypical thinking. And I've never had more friends.*

7. **I Wanted to Stay Numb.** At some level, I understood that my drinking buffered me from negative feelings, scary experiences, and the monotony of life. But in my efforts to escape bad feelings, I was missing out on more and more of the good ones too. *These days I am enjoying the rewards of being present in my own life—for all of it.*

8. **I Was Protecting God's Reputation.** I actually believed this! But of course, God doesn't need protecting from me. Actually, he gets much better press when we get honest about our human failings than when we pretend to be something we're not. *Now I can admit that I was far more worried about my reputation than God's.*

9. **I Thought I Was "Bad," not Sick.** Because I didn't understand alcoholism or addiction in general, I thought I had a moral problem that could be fixed if I just found a way to

mean it when I repented. And why would I reach for outside help if the issue was my sin? *Now I know addiction is a web that traps the whole person. It's sin, but it also a spiritual malady, a mental obsession, and a physical dependency.*

10. **I Hadn't Met Susan Yet.** Because I didn't know anyone in recovery, I pictured such people as dull and sad. Then I met Susan, a hip, funny, creative person—and recovering alcoholic—whose joy was contagious. Her existence gave me hope. *Now I know that the fellowship of recovery is full of fabulous people who laugh far more than they whine or cry.*

11. **I Anticipated Deprivation.** I assumed that recovery was all about what you give up—what you can't do or drink or have. I imagined a life of constant lack, painful craving and endless deprivation. *Now I know that recovery is about adding to your life until it overflows with spiritual adventure, purpose, and passion. Not always, of course, but often!*

12. **I Couldn't Surrender.** So many times I came up to that line—tried to step over it—and failed. Why couldn't I let go? Why couldn't I surrender my will and my life to my loving God? *Now I realize that, for most of us, spiritual surrender doesn't happen until we're totally defeated—utterly convinced that we can't beat addiction on our own.*

Today I participate in a program of recovery that uses the 12 Step approach to finding freedom from addiction. It works. But so does my list here—in the reverse. If you wanna stay stuck, these are your 12 steps.

Here's the cool thing, though. In spite of all this resistance and my own amazing capacity for self-delusion—God still found a way to rescue me. God can do miracles—and for him, they're not even hard!

Son of a Drunk

In two days, my oldest son Noah turns thirty. And I don't know what to say about that. I don't even know what to think about that. It seems wonderful and impossible, and it makes me want to whine about how I'm aging.

But why bother? The real news here is that my *son* is aging. The son I once feared would any day die of drugs or alcohol.

I used to think the only kind of miracles that really mattered were the big, obvious ones that you could see or touch. Growing up, I would badger my mother, "Why doesn't God just do something huge—a *super* big miracle—so everyone will believe that he is real?!"

I thought God was dumb to not think of that.

Now I know miracles are different than what I had in mind as a child. These days, a miracle is the sight of Noah barging through my front door and going straight to the fridge to steal a can of my lemon LaCroix sparkling water—his and my favorite beverage since we both got sober.

(Once, I went to grab a La Croix from *his* fridge, and he said, "Wait! That's mine. I stole it from you fair and square.")

These days, a miracle is the fact that I'm looking forward to having my ex and his wife here in town for Noah's party. They'll stay several days at my mom's house. We'll all eat good food, hang out, and play board games. If recent history is any indication, we'll have a wonderful time.

These days, a miracle is that we'll be joined at my son's party by many sober, positive friends that he's made. (Five years ago, who could have imagined?)

Clearly, the miracles that matter most to me today are the ones where God is so obviously at work redeeming all of our mistakes.

I think Peter would agree with me. Remember how he tried to

walk on water? And for a moment there, he was doing it. And then, right in the middle of the miracle, he got scared and began to sink.

I used to think this story was the only place in the gospels where we learn about a miracle that failed, or that didn't happen all that way. But now I think differently. The way I see it, the *real* ending to Peter's leaving-the-boat story comes later.

It's in the last chapter of John. After Jesus has been crucified, after Peter has denied him three times and is filled with remorse and shame, Peter goes fishing one morning with another disciple. When the risen Jesus suddenly calls out to him from the shore, Peter leaves the boat again.

Only this time, he doesn't care squat about walking on water. Instead, he dives in and swims as fast he can toward Jesus. The only miracle that matters to him now is another chance. I think it's the same for us today.

And yet, when you're in the middle of a second chance so good that it can only be God's doing—which is where I live these days—it's easy to feel afraid. What if it doesn't last? What if I look away? Or what if my son starts to drown?

Then I remember the truth. The real miracles for my son and me aren't about doing life—or even recovery—perfectly. They're in knowing that if we stumble or fall, there's grace enough to catch us. And God will call to us again in the morning.

So my son turns thirty on Sunday. What more do I need to believe that God is real?

Off With Her Head!

I met a friend for dessert at a new restaurant in town. I was taking my first bite of coconut cake when she drew her sword, took off my head, and served it to me on a platter.

Her surprise attack on my integrity—complete with angry accusations and mean assumptions about my motives—hurt. A lot.

Ever had a similar experience? An unexpected blow from a person you love and thought you were safe with?

Why my head was on the plate next to my coconut cake is beside the point of this post. What matters is that she felt angry and betrayed. And I felt scolded and shamed.

Somehow, I always thought that the verse, "Faithful are the wounds of a friend" meant that the friend would "speak the truth in love." Meaning, she'd be self-controlled, thoughtful, and kind *as* she delivered her wounding words.

But what about when your friend wounds by what she says, *and* how says it? Are those wounds faithful too?

Up until I got sober, I couldn't have separated out the two. I would have reacted to my friend's accusations with defensiveness and outrage. I might have made a scene, stomped out of the restaurant, dismissed my friend—and all of her words—forever.

But that's not what happened. Somehow, I managed to stay calm, listen, and gulp down my surprise and hurt. When she finally let me talk, I apologized for what I could. I agreed with her that I had handled a situation poorly. In the parking lot, we hugged as we parted.

What happened next was also new. I didn't go home and curl up in a ball and want to die. Instead, with God's help, I sorted through my feelings. I wrote and I prayed. And I realized that I could receive wounds of truth from my friend—without accepting the shame she attached to their delivery.

Those wounds I will have to forgive.

In the meantime, being wounded by a friend makes me grateful to have one close enough to do that—which wasn't always the case.

Today I have many good friends who hold my heart in their hands. The risk of getting hurt is very real. But it helps to know that I can receive a wound—faithful or not—and it won't be fatal. And because we love each other, no one has to be *wrong*. No one has to be *bad*. No one needs to be *punished*.

We can all keep our heads.

My Least Favorite Self

I woke with a kink in my soul. A hard, tight knot of anxiety that reminded me of when I used to spend mornings filled with regret about something I did or said while drunk the night before.

The drinking part doesn't happen anymore. But I still get what we refer to in recovery as "emotional hangovers."

When I have one, nine times of out ten, I realize that I have been living on the surface of my life. I've once again gotten caught up in striving, mixed motives, controlling behavior, and self-seeking. I've allowed my least favorite version of myself to take over.

Upon recognizing her—my first impulse is always disgust. I hate this part of myself. I want to punch her. Call her terrible names. Offer her up to God's big fat thumb to be squashed.

I used to think this kind of angry reaction showed virtue: *See God? I'm as sick of myself as I know you are.* I considered self-flagellation a sort of victimless crime—no one gets hurt but me. And I deserve it.

But I was wrong on both counts.

The late Brennan Manning writes,

> One of the most shocking contradictions in Christian living is the intense dislike many disciples of Jesus have for themselves. They are more displeased, impatient, irritated, unforgiving, and spiteful with their own short-comings than they would ever dream of being with someone else's. They are fed up with themselves, sick of their own mediocrity, disgusted by their own inconsistency, bored by their own monotony.

The first time I read this paragraph, I was still active in my alcoholism. It described me perfectly. I loathed myself. Today, I'm sad to say that it still describes me more often than I'd like it to. But what *has* changed is that now I know better.

Now I know that when I try to punish myself, I might feel better for having paid a price—but I miss true change and insult God's grace.

Now I know that when I treat myself with vengeance, there *is* another victim—the next person who crosses my path and needs compassion that I don't have and can't give because I refuse to receive it.

Manning suggests that the best antidote to self-hatred is to, "allow the compassion of God to invade our hearts."

That's easier said than done, of course. But I've found that it's the only real cure for my emotional hangovers. As I allow God's tenderness to penetrate my heart instead of shutting it out for shame, I remember the truth about my least favorite self.

She isn't evil so much as forgetful. She forgets to remember that she is utterly beloved by God.

She doesn't need to be slapped. She needs to be hugged.

Open Your Soul Wide and Say, "Ah."

always wanted to be the kind of person who meditates, wears bohemian skirts, and emanates a calm, groovy aura. But for years, whenever I tried to actually do it—nothing happened. I'd find myself distracted by thoughts like, *I've got to remember to scrub my toilet!*

During much of my life as a Christian, disappointing experiences like these convinced me that meditation was a waste of time. Once I got into recovery, cultivating inner peace and serenity was no longer optional. So when Dave and I heard about a conference near us on contemplative prayer—I was ready. That was more than three years ago, and I've been "meditating" ever since.

Before I go on, let me clarify what I mean by contemplative prayer or meditation. Unlike my regular prayers of petition or thanksgiving, in meditative prayer, I'm silent. My only goal is to be present with God in the moment. You could also call it listening prayer, practicing God's presence, or abiding. Some people call it centering prayer.

For me, it works like this. After my morning devotional reading, I sit quietly for ten to twenty minutes. I quiet my mind and open my soul. When my thoughts wander, I use a word or phrase from my reading to bring my focus back to God. Despite the fact that I often get distracted and rarely experience epiphanies, I do this almost every morning and for a few brief moments at intervals throughout the day. Here's why:

1. **It's how I express my trust in God.** Since my default mode is striving, sitting still for ten minutes is an act of faith—a way to physically demonstrate my belief that I'm getting more done by resting in God than I could by racing around.

2. **It's how I improve my day later right now.** If I spend time in contemplation in the morning, it's like I am wearing a path from my heart to God's. Later in the day when I'm casting about for his presence, my spiritual feet more easily find the path.

3. **It's how I invite God to work on me.** Ordinarily, I'm like a patient who keeps trying to tell the doctor how to heal her. But since spiritual transformation is God's work, not mine, silent prayer helps me open my soul wide for God and say, "Ah."

4. **It's how I pray less—and more.** When I meditate in the morning, I find myself praying more often through the day with way fewer words. I invite God's will instead of suggesting what it should feel like or accomplish for me.

5. **It's how my heart hears God.** Being quiet for ten minutes gives God a chance to get a word in edgewise, so to speak. Often, I don't hear a specific message, but my heart knows something new.

6. **It's how I remember that I'm a spiritual being.** In recovery we often remind each other, "You're not a human being having a spiritual experience—you're a spiritual being having a human experience." Listening prayer keeps me connected to this truth.

7. **It's how I feel my feelings.** In the same way I often don't know what I think until I speak or write, I don't always know what I feel until I sit still and listen.

Despite the myriad benefits of meditative prayer, I try not to require anything of this time. Instead of being greedy for good feelings, I try to adopt a posture of surrender to whatever happens. Or doesn't.

If you don't mediate already, I hope some of these ideas might inspire you to try.

The Prodigal's Sister

This morning I'm thinking about my beautiful sister, Katherine. She's my closest friend and biggest fan.

Katherine is three years older than I am. Growing up, she was the first of us siblings (I also have two younger brothers) to find God. From twelve on, she was determined to "save" the rest of our family.

Unfortunately, any appeal Jesus might have had for me was ruined by his misguided association with her. Chalk it up to extreme sibling rivalry on my part. While I secretly wanted what she had, I was ticked off that she'd somehow gotten first dibs on the whole God-loves-me thing. Which might explain what happened .

It began when I was in middle school. I started to sneak into Katherine's bedroom when she was gone. I'd listen to her "corny" Christian albums I was supposed to hate, and I'd read her "stupid" Christian books, and I'd snatch little pieces of God. When at fifteen I finally let Him all the way in, I did so in private and kept it a secret for months. I didn't want my goody-two-shoes sister to think she'd "won."

Today Katherine continues to be an example to me of what it means to follow love. She's the most caring, generous person I know. And yet, much about her life has not gone the way she hoped it would. She's a single mom who battles depression and by her own admission often struggles to know her purpose in life.

I've known for years that Katherine identifies with the elder brother in the prodigal son story Jesus told—and I get it. She always worked hard to do the right, responsible thing, and all she got was overlooked. Yet when her selfish drunk of a sister decides to get sober, people seem fascinated and *she* gets to write a book.

But here's where my sister's story and the parable diverge. The son in the parable refuses to join his brother's celebration even when his father assures him, "You are always with me, and everything I have is yours."

My sister, though, hearing the same speech from our Father, chooses to believe him. If I had a party today to celebrate some success or good turn, my sister would be the first to show up. She'd want to be in the center of things, blowing up balloons, smiling, and truly happy for me.

Writing about this made me wonder for the first time: So where was the prodigal son while his father was outside pleading with his brother for understanding? For that matter, why didn't he find his brother, apologize for being a jerk, and tell him that it wouldn't be a party without him?

I used to always say that I didn't find God so much as I stole him from my sister. But that isn't really true, and it doesn't give credit where credit is due. Lucky for me, my sister shared Jesus with me—freely and generously. I'm so grateful for my sister these days. And though I don't say it often, it's true. Kath, you'll always be the most important person at my party.

"You Listen Like a Man"

One recent evening, Dave and I sat in the living room talking about some issues related to his work. He was struggling to figure out what he was thinking and feeling. So I tried to help him. Isn't that what wives are good for?

A few minutes later, he came in the kitchen while I was unloading the dishwasher and said, "You listen like a man."

Right away, I knew what he meant. He meant that just now I'd been too anxious to fix things and offer helpful opinions when all he'd wanted was for me to listen. The funny thing is, I knew what I was doing even as it was happening. And yet, I felt resistance about Dave calling me out. Just because I had some ideas in response—good ones, I thought—doesn't mean I wasn't listening, does it?

But that's not what matters, I reminded myself. What matters is that Dave didn't feel heard and loved. He probably never finished talking, which would mean that my brilliant insights were not just unasked for, but premature.

I like to think I'm a good listener. But it's listening *without talking* that I can't seem to do very well. Maybe it's because if I only listen, I don't look brilliant. And I don't get that, "Wow I just helped someone!" feeling. I don't get to imagine that I'm in control.

A dear friend is getting ready to file for divorce. I've struggled to know how to help and what to say. Recently, she let slip what she really wants from me. She asked if she could come over and sit in my rocking chair on our porch and watch the world go by. "Porch convalescing," she called it. Imagine—that close to me, and she's not asking for my thoughts?

Poet Mark Nepo mentions an old dear friend who "listens like a lake." I love that image—clear, deep, still. So why do I more often listen like a babbling brook?

Sober Boots

Since I started my writing about recovery, I have never dispensed so many words of advice. So many opinions, definitions, one-liners.

Today, I feel chastened a little about that. A little humbled and hesitant. And I think that's a good thing.

For any one of us, even wise advice has little power until we need it so desperately that we reach for it. Then we can hear it. The truth we're looking for seems to rise up from our souls. God whispers it to us. The solution *dawns* on us.

Sometimes, it even spills out in our own words while a dear friend sits nearby, attentive and still, listening like a lake.

It's Happening Again

It's happening again. Camping with Dave. Fun with Dave. Hikes with Dave. Moon-spotting with Dave.

It's happening without beer to suck down with my feet on the dash as Dave drives.

It's happening without panic that I will run short of alcohol—or worse, Dave might find the wine hidden in my clothing or the big beers hidden nearby in a bush.

It's happening without my waking up with knives in my brain and wondering why I do this—there's so much pain.

It's happening without panic about last night: *Did we fight again? I can't remember.*

It's happening without my needing to put a shield between my lover and me so that I don't know I'm naked.

It's happening without my resenting the hiking that always lasted too long and delayed our return to camp and drinking, which is when the day always really began, and everything before that was just *waiting*.

It's happening without my heart sick with shame and fear and the awful knowing that I am a fraud, a liar, and a sneak. And no matter how much Dave *thinks* he knows me he doesn't really. So he can't really love me.

It's happening *with* the same dog, the same man, the same camper—but nothing is the same or will ever be again. Thank God.

You might think it strange that years later I still reminisce about the terrible times that are no longer happening—but I can't help it. The contrast is still too great, the miracle still too near, and my only fear now is that I might forget.

In all this good living I might think I've changed enough to go back and sip where terror waits, begging me to come.

No thank you. I'm busy. I'm going camping with Dave.

Your Most
Successful Failure

My friend is at the point in her recovery where it's time to try to face the destruction her drinking has brought upon those she loves—and consider how to make amends.

Yesterday, I listened as she stumbled through a long list of people she has lied to, stolen from, abused, neglected, or otherwise forsaken. Her voice shook and her hands trembled as she spoke about her failures.

So would you think me strange if I told you that bearing witness to this was the best thing that's happened to me lately?

For the alcoholic, taking this step requires an insane amount of courage. Every admission feels painful, scary, and embarrassing. But for the person privileged enough to share the moment, it feels like being present for a wild success.

I might quote Brennan Manning too much, but here I go again:

"In my days of wine and roses, sour wine and withered roses, when I was stashing vodka bottles in the bathroom, the glove compartment, and the geranium pot, I saw my life as a complete waste.... It was a long winter of discontent, guilt, fear, shame, and unbearable hypocrisy. The future held out only the bleak prospect of a wet brain and an alcoholic shuffle, commitment to a funny farm, or premature death. The disease meant failure with no redeeming aspect whatsoever. But living out of the center has taught me that every failure succeeds in some way. It provides the opportunity not only to humble the self, but also to be with the failure of others. If your life or mine were an untarnished success story, an unbroken upward spiral toward holiness, we might never come to understand the human heart."

I love this excerpt because it describes so well the despair I felt before I got sober. But it also explains a little about what's been happening to me lately.

As I learn to "be with" the failures of others, the compassion I experience begins to spill over to an area where I probably need it most—toward myself.

Which just might be the wildest success of all.

Almost a
Mother-in-Love

In two days I'm leaving town for Oregon where Dave's oldest son, Neil, *and* my youngest son, Nathan, are getting married a week apart. In their fiancés, Amanda and Kelsey, I am gaining two beautiful, amazing daughters-in-law—or as I heard another woman put it once, "daughters-in-love." This means I'm on the verge of becoming something I always wanted to be—a mother-in-love. I can hardly wait.

And yet, I know from experience that this trip will also challenge me in numerous ways: *I'll miss my routines.* I'm one of those people who covets her little ruts. Life doesn't feel right when I don't get to eat my breakfast of yogurt and berries in front of CNN or take a twenty-minute power nap after lunch.

I'll experience regression.

Yes, much has changed for me. But when my family gets together, I tend to revert to old ways of being that used to work but don't any longer.

I'll encounter tons of relatives. Old relatives! New relatives! Ex-relatives! Fortunately, Dave and I are both fond of all three categories. Still, a collision of past and present is always a bit disorienting and can be fertile ground for conflict.

I'll have to mind my recovery. I go a little insane if I don't take my daily "medicine"—morning time with God, 12-step meetings, and close connection with fellow alcoholics. All these things are more difficult to do when you're traveling.

I'll forget about reality. Seriously. I tend to romanticize a joyful occasion like this one, and without meaning to, I develop all kind of expectations, which set me up for resentments when people don't cooperate. Add to all of this the emotional intensity of such a special occasion—*My baby is getting married, people!*—and you can see why I am carefully preparing for this trip

In the meantime, I asked a recovering friend who has been in crisis—to make a list of women in the program that she felt willing to ask for help, especially while I'm gone. I invited them all to my house for dessert last night, and they showed up in every sense of the word. By the time they left—after much laughing, a little crying, and lots of obvious caring—my friend had filled her day planner with meetings— for lunch, biking, a movie, swimming, or coffee. *Love* appointments.

Of course, I had needed to ask for help just as much as my friend. Something one of the women said stuck with me. She reminded us that we can and should ask each other for help, saying, "None of us can do this thing alone. God is our one, true Source. And we are the *re-Sources* he can use."

Should I
Say Something?

recently got an email from a reader who'd been designated by a group
of friends to confront another friend about her excessive drinking.
Was such a conversation wise, she asked me, and if so, how should she
go about it?

Since I've received several similar emails, I want to address her
question. But with a couple caveats: This isn't about how to do a family
or professional intervention. And it won't be an adequate discussion
for many who are affected deeply and daily by a loved one's addiction.

To start, let's agree that a conversation expressing concern about
another person's behavior is always a risk. It's a rare person—much
less an addict—who responds to that kind of news in a positive way.

Still, there's a place for it—an important one. I like to think that
every expression of genuine concern puts another dent in an addict's
denial that they have a problem. And should tragedy strike, you won't
live with regret that you didn't speak up. Here are my tips for how you
might best show your concern.

Educate yourself. Before you ever speak a word, know something about the particular addiction this person is facing. If
you don't care enough to explore the issue, you might want to
consider whether you care enough to have the conversation.

Assess your motive. Get clarity for yourself about what you're
hoping to achieve, and why. Make sure you're not just looking
for a chance to express your anger or feel morally superior.

Adjust your expectations. It's easy to walk into the conversation with an idealized vision of what will happen. But the

ideal rarely happens. Are you prepared to experience the person's resistance, denials, accusations, anger, or rejection?

Don't speak on behalf of others. "I know your mom is worried, too" doesn't work, even if she is. And speaking as if you represent an unseen majority only makes a person feel ganged up on and ostracized.

Leave diagnosing to the experts. Unless a person uses them first, avoid labels like "alcoholic" or "addicted." Instead, stick to your own observations about their choices and behavior, and the consequences connected to them. Perhaps wonder aloud if they might be more stuck than they realize.

Resist comparisons to Aunt Betty. Every time my mother said, "I worry that you're like Grandma Margie," my resistance only stiffened. It might be okay to point out a possible genetic vulnerability, but it's rarely helpful to ask the person to identify with a negative example.

Identify with the struggle. If you can't relate to the specific drug or activity, you might say: "I haven't struggled with alcohol, but boy have I struggled with ____." Or if you don't relate at all, simply admit, "I can't imagine how hard this kind of thing must be."

Avoid arguing about details. How often they're drunk, how much they eat, how many people they slept with, isn't the point. Let them talk about the issue in their own way, and look for your opportunity to say the one or two things you came to say: "I'm so worried." Or, "You're choices scare me."

Remember that shaming backfires. If this person has embarrassed or betrayed you or themselves, they probably already know it. Focus on the facts rather than on your own value judgments. Most addicts are already so bound up by shame that adding to it only drives them further into self-hatred, which drives them closer to their drug of choice for relief.

Don't treat a person's potential addiction as if it's a sin issue only. If you're talking to a Christian, chances are they've already tried repentance and prayer. Instead of asking them to try harder at something that hasn't worked, invite them to consider that God might be asking them to seek outside help.

Be prepared with a do-able next step. It only took one phone call to set me into motion away from habitual drunkenness and toward healing. Go prepared with contact information for a local person-in-the-know, professional organizations, or programs that might offer the right kind of help. Or if the person is willing, promise that you will walk with them step-by-step to find it.

Bring closure to the discussion. If you sense the person isn't ready to deal with your concern, you might agree not to bring this up again. Otherwise, set up a time when you'll check in. Assure them your talk hasn't changed how much you like or love them. Avoid the kind of vague ending that will leave you both feeling awkward.

However your friend responds, you've done a beautiful thing. Try not to rehash things in your mind too much. If you strongly feel like you blew it—lost your temper or got manipulative, for example—do what we recovering addicts do. Make amends...and set about with gratitude to do the next right thing.

"No One Will Know If I Eat This Cake" (The 12 Lies of Relapse)

I t doesn't matter whether you're recovering from an addiction to food, drugs, alcohol, pornography, shopping, or power—temptation will come knocking. Unfortunately, it won't be dressed in red or have a pointy tail. That would make it too easy.

Instead, for most of us, the invitation to indulge our compulsions sounds like the voice of reason in our head. Next time you feel tempted, see if you can't recognize one of these twisted lies in your thinking—and combat it with the truth instead:

1. **The Lie of Deprivation:** "I'm missing out on something good." The Truth: *I am not being deprived, but spared, since my substance or activity of choice has become like poison to me.*

2. **The Lie of Identity:** "I'm a sex (or relationship) addict, so of course I sleep around." The Truth: *My addiction doesn't define who I am, but only something I used to do.*

3. **The Lie of Entitlement:** "After the day I've had, I deserve this!" The Truth: *My addiction is not a reward, but a form of self-punishment, since it leads to misery and regret.*

4. **The Lie of Secrecy:** "No one will know if I eat this entire cake." The truth: *I will know it, and so will God, and we're who matter most.*

5. **The Lie of Minimization:** "If I only take a bite/sip/look, it's no big deal." The Truth: *What matters isn't the amount; if I try to cheat and violate my conscience, I'm relapsing.*

6. **The Lie of Control:** "If I binge today, I can always repent and get right back on the wagon tomorrow." The Truth: *Every time I fall off the wagon, it gets harder to climb back on—and stay on.*

7. **The Lie of Self-pity:** "No one cares how hard I'm trying to change, so why bother?" The Truth: *I'm not in recovery to impress or gain kudos but to live true to myself.*

8. **The Lie of Inevitability:** "I'm going to relapse sooner or later. Might as well be now." The Truth: *Relapse does not have to be part of my recovery story. I never have to act on that compulsion again.*

9. **The Lie of Change:** "Look how far I've come—I think I can handle a single drink now!" The Truth: *No matter how much I have grown, I am never cured of my addiction.*

10. **The Lie of Revenge:** "Fine! Take that! I'll just get high and you'll be sorry." The Truth: *If I use my addiction as a weapon, I'm the one who will be hurt first—and probably the most.*

11. **The Lie of Unworthiness:** "I don't deserve to be sober, happy, and free in recovery. I've hurt too many people." The Truth: *Recovery is a gift of grace that no one earns but anyone may receive. Plus, staying sober is how I make a living amends.*

12. **The Lie of Crisis:** "This is just too much for me to handle—everyone will understand if I turn to my addiction now." The Truth: *When life hurts, I don't have to reach for my drug of choice. With the comfort and support of my community, my recovery program, and my God, I can handle this!*

One of my favorite sayings in recovery goes to this last point: "There is no problem that drinking or _____, (fill in the blank) can't make *worse*."

I should tell you that this list is not the slightest bit scientific. These particular lies occurred to me because I've met them all roaming the dangerous, dark streets of my mind. When I relapsed after six months, it was 1, 8, and 10 that ganged up and took me down.

What if the Prodigal Son Relapsed?

I got an email from a woman who relapsed after staying sober for almost two years. I'll call her Anna.

Anna didn't say why she relapsed. But she did say that the lies I listed in my piece about relapse sounded familiar to her.

All of them.

"I tell myself all twelve of these almost every day," Anna wrote. "After 21 months of sobriety, I have turned into a chronic relapser. Yuck. And it gets harder each time. The quitting drinking gets harder. The sobering up is harder. The steps are harder. Everything..."

Anna's note got me thinking about what happens *after* you relapse. That sick feeling you have in the pit of your stomach. The guilt, shame, and even shock: *How, after being rescued by God, forgiven by loved ones, cheered on by friends—could I have thrown it all away again?*

You're probably familiar with Jesus' parable about a prodigal son who squanders his inheritance on the party life until he's broke, starving, and envies the pigs he's been hired to feed. In one of the gospel's most beautiful moments, he arrives home to the open arms of a loving father who fully re-instates him—no good thing withheld.

But what if, after all of that, the prodigal son relapsed? What if he helped himself to more of his father's cash (or maybe his brother's) and started out on that journey to the pigs all over again?

Imagine how his thoughts might go: *You're a hopeless loser who will never learn; you can never go home again, so you might as well keep this party going; Wait! Maybe you should just kill yourself—you'd all be better off...*

Recognize any of these? I do, too. That's because after our inner addict celebrates our fall with a victory dance, her next concern is how to keep the food, drink, drugs, or sex coming. That means—you guessed it—*more lies*. Plus, you've just handed her some great new material to work with.

In my experience, most of the lies you hear *after* a relapse share the same aim: To make you feel too ashamed, afraid, or discouraged to try to recover again.

In other words, they'll be lies about *you*. And lies about *God*.

I wonder, if the prodigal son returned again a second or third time, would he receive the same reception from his father? Since we don't know if Dad was in Alanon, we can't be sure. :-)But wouldn't you agree that the *son's* answer to this question—what he expected— would likely determine whether he decided to make his home in the mud or with his father?

I think it's that way with us, too. What we believe about God's love for us has a lot to do with whether, or how quickly, we recover from the heartbreak of relapse.

Given this, I wonder if Jesus told the prodigal story especially for addicts—otherwise known as humans. He knew we'd struggle to wrap our mind around the inexhaustible nature of God's mercy. He wanted us to know that our Father is ready to forgive before we even repent— even if it's for the tenth time.

As soon as we rise from the mud and turn, he is already running to meet us.

"I Can Do it Myself!"

The first time I encountered the concept of powerlessness in recovery, I didn't get it.

"No one forces the glass to my lips," I objected. "And even if I *was* powerless, how would admitting that I can't not drink help me not to drink?

It made no sense.

Then one day I was sitting in a recovery meeting when a big burly man who'd spent twelve years in prison spoke about his great relief at admitting he was powerless. He said he was finally willing to let God do for him what he couldn't do for himself.

His comment made me flash back to scenes with my son when he was a toddler. Long before he had a clue how to tie his shoes, he fought off my help. "I can do it myself!" he'd insist. He pitched a similar fit when I wouldn't let him pour his own milk on his cereal and all over the table.

Those memories helped me see something: How often I get in God's way when he's trying to help. How God can't do for me what I insist on doing for myself.

Since that day I've come to recognize my powerlessness over alcohol. First, I had to admit that I couldn't have one drink and stop. Second, I had to admit that I'd never been able to resist that first drink. Sound powerless enough for you?

Still, I continue to be amazed at how stubborn and self-willed I am (my son got it from somewhere). I know very well that I need God's power, but when I face a stiff challenge, I almost always reach for my own strength first.

It's baffling, isn't it? Why not *start* with dependence on God instead of having to first exhaust our own efforts?

It should be simple, but it's not. And lately, I think I'm discovering part of the reason why. I don't rely on myself because I think I'm stronger or smarter than God, but because I want to feel *in control*. I trust God to help me, but I'd rather he let me lead the way and lend his strength.

In other words, I'm willing to let God be my higher power as long as he does *my* will.

Which explains some of my initial confusion about how admitting powerlessness frees us from addiction: *On it's own it doesn't.* If you stop after Step One, "Admitted we were powerless over alcohol,…" all that's changed is that you now have an excuse.

Step Two brings more hope: "Came to believe that God could restore us to sanity." But still, it's not enough to believe God *can* do this. We have to *let* him (the control issue again).

Which is where the genius of Step Three comes in: "Turned our will and our life over to the care of God." Here is where I take the action that solves the problem of powerlessness I admitted in Step One.

But how does surrendering my will give me power?

Here's how I think it works. In addiction, we act against our own will—and we're astonishingly powerless to resist. But when we surrender our determination to stay in control and do what we want in exchange for God's will for us, we open our lives to his power, *because his power always flows in the direction of his will.*

Today, I'm so thankful God is ready to help us do any hard thing he places in our path if we'll only let him. Plus, he's more patient than the best mother. He lets us try until we finally see we can't do it on our own. Then, he gently takes our hands in his and helps us to pour our milk and tie our shoes.

Sometimes he even whispers what my son always wanted to hear: *Good job!*

"They Come in Droves"

Eight years ago, when Dave and I first moved into our circa 1890s house in Colorado Springs, the neighbors warned us about Halloween. Apparently, our Victorian-era neighborhood was a big trick-or-treating destination. And we could see why. With its spook-ready architecture, enormous trees (lots of fall leaves to kick through), old-fashioned lamp posts, and light traffic on wide streets, our part of town is pretty much goblin heaven.

"They come in droves," one neighbor told us.

We should have asked her to define "droves." We figured it probably meant dozens, and prepared accordingly.

But before that first Halloween night was over, Dave had made three emergency runs to Safeway for more candy. Apparently, droves means *h-u-n-d-r-e-d-s*.

I had never seen so many trick-or-treaters in my life, and such original costumes! The Energizer Bunny with his drum, the ghost of Raggedy Ann, a jumbo box of Crayola crayons, bee babies, angels, pirates…they all charged our door that night, buckets and bags in hand, in a line that stretched out to the sidewalk. At moments, it felt like mayhem.

And yet, when things finally settled down at around 9—it was a school night, after all—I was sad to see it end.

The next morning, out for a walk with Edmund, we saw signs of Halloween-past everywhere. A pirate's scarf stuck on our fence post. A Kit Kat on the walkway.

"When I went to the gym earlier," Dave said, "I saw glittering angel wings blowing down the street."

I imagined an angel from the night before—now waking up, just a little girl again. I wondered how she lost her wings, and if her parents promised to make her new ones for next year.

Later that day, I came upon the familiar verse in Hebrews that invites us to, "Come boldly to the throne of grace so we can find help in our time of need." I had always loved that passage, but now the word "boldly" struck me as a stretch.

Did God *really* want me to approach him with that kind of audacity? Like I expect something good—even now? You see, this was also my first year in recovery. And just two weeks before Halloween, I had suffered a relapse—gotten angry at Dave and drank at him.

Lately, I was more inclined to approach God like Edmund approaches me after he's gotten into the garbage again—skulking, ears back with guilt.

Then I remembered all those kids from the night before. How confidently they had come tromping up to our door. None of them came because they thought they *deserved* our candy. They came because they knew we *wanted* them to come, *hoped* they'd come.

Surely, that's how it is with God, too, I decided. God doesn't care how spectacularly we've failed, or how recently we've lost our wings.

I don't know what Halloween looks like where you live. But I hope it involves lots of excited kids. And I hope they remind you to storm God's door, breathless with a good kind of greed for a grace more generous than you could possibly deserve.

The Relief of
Not Enough

I t was another truly magical Halloween evening. Mild weather.
Families strolling together. Cameras flashing. The happy sound of
children's laughter.

We bought enough candy for at least a thousand kids. Still, by
7:30, we were already running low. Dave raced to the store for more—
but it wasn't enough. We ended up having to shut down early, around
8:30. It totally bummed me out.

Back inside the house, a friend reminded me that it was no big
deal. "So what if you ran out of candy," she said. "Those kids are getting plenty!" I knew she was right, but still . . .

Later, I realized that my dismay had less to do with kids or candy,
and more to do with my frequent fear of coming up short, not having
enough, or not being enough for someone else. It's a human thing, I
know. None of us like to disappoint.

But sometimes I wonder if addicts aren't more prone to feel this
way. Maybe when you live for so long trying and failing to ever *get*
enough, it's hard to believe for a moment that you could ever *give*
enough.

I ran across this gem from poet Mark Nepo: "In a deep and subtle
way, the want to *do* it all is a want to *be* it all (emphasis mine)."

Oh my, he's right, I thought. My problem is not that I don't feel like
enough, it's that in trying to be enough for you, I start to play God. I
forget that the gap between what I have to offer and what you really
need is the sacred space where God gets to show up in your life. It's
a spiritual paradox for sure. On the one hand I know that I *am* more
than enough. How could it be otherwise when I am made in the image
of the living God and in Christ I am heir to every spiritual blessing?

But I also know that apart from God, I am *not* enough—no one is. And if I try to feed my ego by becoming all things to all people, I make myself miserable.

I understand why some people find value in chanting a mantra such as, "I am enough! I am more than enough!" I might try that sometime myself. But I'm learning that there's relief, too, in accepting that I am also *not* enough—and was never meant to be. I can take a deep breath and rest in my own limitations, knowing that where I end is where God can begin. Today, that sounds like plenty.

Pick a Chair:
AA or Celebrate Recovery?

Now and then, I get emails from readers who wonder whether I recommend Alcoholics Anonymous or Celebrate Recovery. My answer is always the same: *It all depends*. I know people in both programs who have experienced the miracle of long-term recovery. I also know plenty of people who tried one or the other and didn't like it, so they switched. Both programs base their approaches on Christian principles. But there are important differences:

AA is the original source of the now widely used 12 Steps. CR uses a revised version of the 12 Steps and 8 Principles based on the Beatitudes. AA's main text is the book, *Alcoholics Anonymous*, while CR has its own Bible-based curriculum.

AA takes an inclusive approach to God, encouraging people to rely on a God of their own understanding, often referred to as a "higher power." CR teaches that Jesus Christ as revealed in the Bible is the only true path to God. AA and its sister groups, such as NA (Narcotics Anonymous) or OA (Overeaters Anonymous), focus on specific addictions.

CR is broader, and it addresses all kinds of "hurts, habits, and hang-ups." AA considers itself a recovery program and avoids promoting any single religion or faith tradition. CR describes itself as a ministry, and is unapologetically evangelical. (If you don't know Jesus, they want to introduce you.)

Not surprisingly, both Alcoholics Anonymous and Celebrate Recovery have plenty of vocal proponents, some who honestly believe theirs is the only right or effective path to lasting recovery. But I have seen that God works through both programs. In fact, I'm convinced that God is so eager to rescue and heal that he will rush to the aid of any addict who cries out to him for help, regardless of what room they're sitting in. But if you need to choose, how might you proceed? Consider: CR might work best for you if:

- Christian doctrine is of first importance to you, especially with regard to your recovery.
- You enjoy an evangelical Christian atmosphere that may include community worship as part of the program.
- You prefer a gender-specific approach, where men and women always attend separate groups.
- You're most relaxed when surrounded by like-minded people who generally share your beliefs and values.
- You view addiction as a spiritual and moral problem, not a disease.

AA might work best for you if:

- You don't mind sitting next to people who don't share your moral convictions or faith beliefs (and who may use foul language on occasion).
- You welcome the chance to encounter familiar spiritual truths in a fresh way.
- You'd rather not attend recovery groups with the same people you worship next to on Sunday.
- You see a secular recovery setting as an opportunity to serve and love people who might never darken the door of a church.
- You believe addiction is not only a spiritual and moral problem, but also a disease.

I know—my list is somewhat arbitrary and incomplete, and anyone could argue with it. But I'm going out on a limb here because I want those who suffer to know what options are available and that both these programs can be found in almost every community in North America.

If you are looking for help, consider trying both groups, maybe more than once. Keep in mind that each meeting will have its own flavor and doesn't necessarily reflect the larger program. Sometimes, proximity or schedule will limit your choices. But the best fit is always the one you can attend on a regular basis. (Maybe, like some people I know, you'll choose to attend both!) Of course, you're no more likely to find a perfect recovery program than you are a perfect church. And even if you did, once you showed up, it would no longer be perfect, right?

The first time I went to a recovery meeting, I was convinced that it was the worst thing that could ever happen to me. It turned out to be the best.

So pick a chair, why don't you? Somewhere, God is saving a seat for you.

Gratitude
and a Girl Like Me

When I first got into recovery for my alcoholism, I couldn't understand the constant emphasis on gratitude. What did a "thank you" sent God's way or feeling appreciation for my blessings have to do with *not* drinking?

Today, I not only get the connection, I'm convinced that our ability to experience long-term recovery is directly related to our ability to live in gratitude.

What changed my mind? For starters, I got really thirsty in early sobriety. I felt deprived, angry, and I desperately wanted to drink. I was forced to face the question: How do you turn off craving? How do you shut down desire? How do you satisfy that endless ache?

I found the largest part of my answer in gratitude. It makes sense when you think about it: Addiction is all about the greedy pursuit of something we desperately want and can't get enough of. It always leads to feelings of deprivation and discontent. Gratitude is all about the humble pursuit of appreciation for the good we already have. It almost always leads to feelings of abundance and contentment.

To my way of thinking, the opposite of addiction isn't sobriety, but gratitude. Sounds easy enough, right? And it is—*if* you're talking about gratitude merely as a form of politeness, a box to check, or a passing appreciation for obvious blessings.

But for those of us suffering from serious addictions—especially in moments of painful craving or deep discontent—turning the tide toward thankfulness is no easy task. Merely telling ourselves, "You should be grateful," usually doesn't help. We agree in our heads…and feel twice as bad for it.

I've found that it helps to understand that gratitude isn't a feeling that *happens to* me. It's an intentional posture I choose to adopt. It's a stance I take in my soul toward the world. It's a way of seeing that helps me experience all the good that comes to me as sheer gift. For me, it's a spiritual practice that looks something like this.

In the morning, I ask God to empty my heart of expectations I might have about my day. I remember that I'm not entitled to have things go my way. I anticipate the day ahead and how I might give to others, because nothing makes you feel rich and thankful quicker than being generous.

As the day unfolds, I pause often to touch home base in my soul. I shut my eyes or take several deep breaths. I shake loose of my impulse (and it's wicked strong) to control the world around me. I relax and invite God to redirect the eyes of my soul toward grace.

Some days, I accomplish all this in a simple, two-word prayer. *Thank you.* Other days, it takes more conscious, intentional work to stay in a grateful frame of mind. And more days than I like—*let's be honest here!*—I'm just too tired, distracted, or lost in self-pity to even try for thankfulness.

Still, I think gratitude is supposed to be somewhat elusive. I think we're supposed to break our hearts a bit looking for it. Of all my many blessings, I'm *most* thankful for a simple, growing capacity to *cherish* and *experience* gratitude. Not as a duty or a flattering virtue I pretend to possess, but as a spiritual posture I get to adopt that leaves me feeling *content.* Not thirsty. Not desperate for more. Craving nothing but grace. For a girl like me, that's a miracle.

Flight Lessons

On Sunday, Dave decided to take our grown kids for an afternoon drive to the top of nearby Pikes Peak. Since I couldn't imagine anything less fun (I'm not a fan of twisty roads with steep drop-offs and no guardrails), I decided to go to a movie instead.

I'd heard that *Flight*, starring Denzel Washington, was a great movie about a seasoned pilot who, ironically enough, pulls off an amazing act of daring and skill while dangerously under the influence. I figured his story might provide some fodder—a pithy line of dialogue or a compelling insight—for my writing.

I forgot that the best fodder comes from *personal experience*. And that a good movie isn't only about the main character's story, but yours too.

As a point of pride (watch out for those!), I never cry at movies. I don't like being emotionally manipulated. Plus, my mother cries at movies. My sister cries, too. I like to think I'm a more evolved and sophisticated viewer. *Right.* I sobbed all the way home in heavy traffic and bright sunshine.

At first, I couldn't explain my reaction. And then, it dawned on me that the movie had managed to take me back in time to those last miserable weeks of my drinking: The lying. The hiding. The shame. The terror that all of it wouldn't end—or worse, that it would. I couldn't imagine any version of sobriety then that didn't sound like hell.

But that wasn't why I was crying, I realized. I was crying from the deep relief of knowing that I don't ever have to go back there again, combined with heartbreak for those who still haven't found a way out.

Previously, I wrote about gratitude as a spiritual posture that you can intentionally adopt. Watching *Flight* reminded me that gratitude can also arrive as a gift that has nothing to do with you. It catches you by surprise, like a sharp intake of breath.

On the way home from that movie, I saw things more clearly. I realized that what matters is that I understand that until further notice, writing for people who struggle with addiction is my *calling*, and a sacred privilege. Very practically speaking, it's how I breathe in gratitude, and breathe it out again. It's how I keep myself from drowning in the backwash of my own blessings.

Addiction can at times feel like a crummy assignment. Some days, recovery doesn't add up. Hope washes away. People get sober only to go back out and drink. Friends die. Marriages crash. Careers go down in vomit. And no one ever gets forever cured.

Some days, I don't know what to make of it all. I don't understand how life works. I don't know much of anything. Except that I have to breathe. And I don't think I can do that unless I do what I can to help others.

What if You're Doing Better Than You Think?

One of the hazards of recovery—and probably Christianity, too—is that we get so focused on change and growth that we forget that we're okay right now. God isn't waiting for us to finally get it all together so he can love us more.

Not long ago, I was helping a friend do some step work around a snarly job situation that had spawned a snake's nest of resentments. As we talked through her anger at others, her part in it all started coming at her fast and furious: Ego. Pride. Denial. Compromise.

My friend was in tears, disappointed and scared. "How could this have happened when I've been trying so hard?" There she was, sitting across the table from me, face scrunched with crying, all her pages of writing spread out between us. And in that moment, I thought I caught a glimpse of God's compassion for her—how completely precious her sincere struggle was to him.

"Look at you!" I said, sitting back. "Do you see yourself? Look how hard you're trying. Taking hours out of your busy day to do this work—all because you want to grow and live in God's will and help others. I think you're totally amazing, and so does he. You've never been a more beautiful person than you are right now."

She gazed at me with at least a little doubt.

"No, really," I said, plunging ahead. "God's not waiting for you to finally lick all these things or get it all together. Guess what? That will never happen! This is it. You're doing it. The stumbling forward, falling back, wobbling this way and that—this is life. It's how God made us, and it's okay."

"Oh my God...you're right!" she said finally. She heaved a sigh, and started scribbling notes, trying to capture what I'd just said.

On the way home in the car, I couldn't help wishing someone would say those words to me. I related a little too closely to my friend's situation—where you think you've got some shortcoming licked, only to have it kick your butt again.

An hour later, I opened an email from a reader and saw that she'd included a quote:

"What if it's all okay? What if we're all doing better than we could ever imagine? What if God is pleased with us even on our most ordinary, ego-driven days? What if this is simply what it looks like to be a human being on earth and we should all worry less? What if there's nothing we need to necessarily FIX today? What a shame if we all run around living in FIX-it mode—only to discover that we could have relaxed into God instead and let ourselves be okay with being a bit broken?"

I was halfway through the quote before I realized that I'd recently written these words in another piece and then promptly forgot them. Now my reader was quoting them back to me. Oh, the kindness—and good humor—of God! Clearly, he'd been humming around my heart, giving me words for my friend in advance of her needing them. And now, he wanted to make sure I got the message, too.

I read it again, slowly, and I saw the words ricochet—from God through me to the reader and then back again to lodge in my heart.

I thought you might also need to hear them today.

This Could Be Me

t's a beautiful, snowy morning here in Colorado. Dave went to church. I've been sick these past few days, so I stayed home.

I just ate a late breakfast of yogurt, berries, and granola and turned on the TV to watch CNN while I ate.

The news troubled me. The top story was about a Dallas Cowboys player, Jerry Brown Jr., who was killed early this morning in a drinking and driving accident. His teammate, Josh Brent, was driving—and is being charged with his death.

These stories always stir up a mix of feelings for me. First, horror. Then grief for the families. Then relief that it wasn't me driving drunk—quickly followed by a flash of shame that it could have been.

I did that. During my drinking years, I drove under the influence on many occasions. Worse, I drove to meet my ex-husband over snowy mountain passes while drinking Seagram's wine coolers out of a diet coke can *with my kids in the car.*

Because the drive was boring.

I know, it's incomprehensible. Inexcusable. What was I thinking!?

But I wasn't, of course. Thinking and drinking rarely happened at the same time for me, which was part of the problem.

Now you can see why whenever I see a news story like this, I say under my breath, "But for the grace of God there go I . . . ."

But this morning, I noticed how casually this phrase rolled out. And it bothered me. What do I really mean by that? Am I really willing to identify myself with someone who has committed such a monstrous act of selfishness?

This morning, I am.

Or at least, I'm trying to. As an ex-drunk-driver who simply never got caught, in some way—even beyond symbolically—I share in the blame every time a blitzed driver kills someone.

I did what this guy did—just with different consequences.

Maybe what I really want to say this morning is, *I'm sorry.* I am so sorry that I endangered your children and your loved ones. I'm sorry that I behaved so selfishly and recklessly. I'm sorry that an apology is all I have to offer.

Recently I read a blog where a guy was questioning why alcoholics in recovery keep getting together and talking about it, over and over: *Get over it!* He urged. *Just solve the problem, shut up, and move on!*

But what if we did? What if once we got sober, we quit meetings? Who would be there for the newcomer? Who would be sitting in that room when the would-be future drunk-driving killer of your child gets sentenced to recovery meetings for a DUI?

If at all possible, I will be there. For the rest of my life, I hope, I will try to pass on the miracle of freedom given to me. How could I do anything less?

Recovery saves lives, people. It's not a feel-good club. It's not only about self-help. *It's also a gathering of would-be drunk drivers who have seen the error of their ways and want to save lives.*

But for the grace of God . . . there go I.

5 Ways to Change Your Past

I know, I know. They say you can't improve your past and it's a waste of time trying. But I'm here to tell you that I've seen it happen. I offer Wendy as proof.

On Tuesday, I picked her up to drive her to a meeting. She looked radiant as she explained in a rush of words how thrilled she was that earlier in the day she got to go speak about alcoholism to a group of soldiers at nearby Fort Carson.

She said she couldn't wait to do it again.

It might not sound like much, but here's what you need to know. For thirteen years, Wendy had a prestigious career as an exercise physiologist in the military. During that time, she tried very hard to hide her severe drinking problem.

"My greatest fear," she once told me, "was that my work would find out."

Five years ago, at the height of her career, she hit and injured a motorcyclist while under the influence. She lost her driver's license, served six months in jail, and spent four more years under the strict supervision of the Department of Corrections.

Naturally, the local paper reported the story. As an indirect result, things soured for Wendy at work and her stellar career in the military was ruined. Since then, just the sight of anyone in uniform could trigger symptoms of posttraumatic stress.

As if to add insult to injury, the summer after losing her job, Wendy had to have knee surgery that kept her immobile for months.

I met Wendy at the height of her crisis. She was what you'd call a hot mess. But all that summer long, while she was laid up, we spent many hours in her sunny back yard, carefully working through the 12 steps.

And it has paid off. As of last month, the courts are no longer supervising Wendy. And she's about to get her driver's license again.

But in some ways, what happened on Tuesday is an even bigger deal. There was a time Wendy wouldn't have believed me if I told her that one day she would not only visit a military campus and tell her story to a room filled with soldiers, she'd love every second of it.

This is what redemption looks like. And the good news is that anyone can do what Wendy did, not just people in recovery.

The way I see it, she did five important things:

1. *She cleaned up her side of the street.* That means she did all she could to make things right—to fix what she'd broken or restore what she'd taken.
2. *She forgave those she might have blamed for her misfortunes.* By taking responsibility for her part in events, she was able to let go of resentments and stop seeing herself as a victim.
3. *She refused to wallow in guilt and shame.* Having made a sincere change of direction, she chose to accept forgiveness rather than try to earn it through punishing herself.
4. *She cooperated with a redemptive plan.* She made herself available, asked God to use her, and agreed in advance to say yes.
5. *She refused to paint her past entirely black.* She held onto the memories of the good that happened even in the darkest times—proof that God didn't wait for her to get sober before he showed up to love her. And the bad memories? They're real, of course, but she tries to visit them only to remind herself of where she never wants to go again.

This is what I mean by improving your past.

Obviously, none of us can alter events that have already happened. But we don't have to go through life feeling like permanent losers because of our failures. We can change our *experience* of the past—then let it motivate us to make a brighter future for ourselves and others.

And that's a *huge* improvement.

A Gathering of Beings

've been thinking about how much we need other people to help us to see ourselves as God does. Which led me to the topic of community. Which led me back to the house in Central Oregon where Dave and I lived before we moved to Colorado.

We bought the place not because it was grand or flashy, but because it had a view of the entire Cascade Mountain Range from the back deck. Much to our surprise, though, we found ourselves enjoying the front yard more.

Out front, between the house and road, the spacious yard was home to a stand of six or eight towering pines. The trees seemed arranged like family—not quite planned, but not quite random either. We got the sense around those big old cinnamon trunks that they had been convening in our grass for years, and *for a reason*—to commune, maybe, or to bear witness to something remarkable, or simply to stand silently in each other's presence. We'd park our Adirondack chairs in their midst after a day's work, lean back, gaze up through the branches, and feel strangely nurtured deep inside.

We decided they were not ordinary trees, but souls. We began to refer to them as our Gathering of Beings. After moving to Colorado, we didn't miss the house or the expensive view all that much, but we did miss the Gathering. It had helped to shelter us through what we later came to realize had been the hardest years of my marriage (the final years of my drinking).

I think a recovery group is like that Gathering of Beings. You can tell we have something more to do with each other than meets the eye. Something about the way we listen and nod at each other hints at a deeper story; it says that we're not here by chance. It's says that we're a *community*. But of course, community is not a recovery thing, it's a human thing. I think you could safely say there are three kinds of people in the world:

- Those who are part of a community.
- Those who are looking for community.
- Those who don't know they're looking for community.

Which kind would you say describes you today?

While I was still drinking, I was in the last category. Definitely. I was so out of touch with my own soul that I had no idea how desperately I longed to belong to others—to be part of something bigger than me.

These days, I feel safe in my recovery group—not because I can hide, but because I can't. It's a place where I'm encouraged to give as well as get. It's a place where I don't have to perform but I am invited to participate. There I commune. I bear witness to miracles. I live in Presence.

Of course, not every room or program with a bunch of people in it is a community. When it's a crowd but not a gathering, you get lonely. Some of you are still searching for that special place—a church, a fellowship, a group where you can experience a connection of souls. I hope you keep looking.

Here's a thought: Maybe God is inviting you to create your own gathering of beings—others who will convene, and listen, and bear witness with you—right where you are. Maybe you're standing in the place you've been looking for all your life.

When Dreams
are Overrated

Years ago I worked on a parable-driven book called *The Dream Giver*. It's about how to find your Big Dream and overcome the obstacles you will inevitably face on your journey.

It's an important message I still believe in: When we identify and pursue what we're put on earth to do, our lives have more purpose. We help more people. Big dreams give us drive.

But they can drive us crazy too—maybe even rob us blind.

Poet Mark Nepo observes:

> "Very often, we define ourselves by what we want or dream of. I want to be an actor or a musician or a president or a grandmother. Yet when our lives shape us differently, we often think we have failed, that we are settling for less, because we weren't good enough to become or have what we wanted."

His words make me think of a friend I have who is a dancer. That artistic identity is what is most dear to her—it's who she is. Yet her circumstances prevent her from pursuing dance fulltime. And even if they didn't, she's not sure her talent is outstanding enough to carry her to professional success.

Which leaves her asking, "But if I can't be a dancer, what's my special thing?"

Subtext: "*Am I worth anything?*"

Sometimes I wonder if dreams aren't overrated.

We've all heard the slogan: *If you can dream it, you can achieve it.* But is that really true? If it is, at what cost? If I can't even define my dream for you, am I a loser? And if my dream fails, have I failed?

Nepo proposes that a dream isn't always meant to be permanent.

"It tends to serve its purpose in our development and then fade away." That's a helpful idea. It suggests that a dream is not so much a destination God has in mind as a boat that can carry us further down the river of his will for our life. It suggests that dreams are more like living prayers than fixed promises or guarantees.

So yes, we should dream. Dreams stretch our imagination, help us explore our gifts, and challenge us to rely on God rather than ourselves. They add color to the world. Sometimes, they change it.

Hopefully, they change *us*.

But if we think a dream gives ultimate meaning to our life or is the only thing that makes us special, we're listening to our ego, not God. And if we measure our happiness by the success of our big dream, we'll miss the irreplaceable gift of being present here and now.

Worst case scenario? *We achieve the dream without the One who gave it to us.*

Toward the end of The Dream Giver parable, the main character—Ordinary—makes a momentous decision. Having finally overcome every obstacle to his Big Dream, Ordinary senses that God is asking him to give it back. He's understandably devastated.

After much anguished wrestling, Ordinary writes one last entry in his dream journal: "I am surrendering my Dream to you, Dream Giver. I've decided that it's you that I can't go on without."

This Makes Sense

love this part of a poem by Hafiz called "Wanting our life to make sense."

> All day long you do this, and then even in your
> sleep. . . *pan for gold.*
> We are looking to find something to celebrate
> with great enthusiasm,
> wanting all our battles and toil and our life to
> make sense."

So, so true. And I am one of those gold-panners, sifting every experience, every thing I read, what other say . . . for that nugget of truth that might buy me some wisdom or help me on my way somehow.

But of course, at the same time, I am not content just to pile up the nuggets somewhere in my head or heart, I want them all to fit together like an expensive lego structure so that it will all make sense–something about the symmetry and timing and truth of my life will add up to Meaning with a capital M.

Why is it some of us are so bent on Meaning and other people are content just to live and be and accept what comes or else label it good or bad, but have no need to think much beyond that? Why do some of us hanker for mystery only to stomp our feet when it doesn't pan out in a way that helps us?

This poem piece dovetailed well with what I read in Frederick Buechner's reflections:

> "'Every morning when you wake up, before you reaffirm your faith in the majesty of a loving God, before you say *I believe* for another day, read the *Daily News* with its record of the latest crimes and tragedies of mankind and then see if you can honestly say it again:

'He was a fool in the sense that he didn't or wouldn't or couldn't resolve, intellectualize, evade, the tensions of his faith but lived those tensions out, torn almost in two by them at times. His faith was not a seamless garment but a ragged garment with the seams showing, the tears showing, a garment that he clutched about him like a man in a storm."'

I love this. And I so relate to that feeling of wearing a faith that has so many holes and is so poorly made that it feels at times embarrassing. And yet, you couldn't rip it off my body or take it away from me for the world. It is all I have to clothe me some days, this tattered silly faith in a God who won't make the world make sense or give it concrete, permanent Meaning, but who insists that I love it anyway.

I'm very aware of things not making sense today, of the injustices of the world, of the unfairness of things—all my blessings and all those blessings that people I love don't have.

And the blessings aren't transferable. They aren't material, but relational and spiritual and circumstantial. Which is part of the problem with being rich with the kind of gold that isn't salable—you can't give it to others even when you want to.

It belongs to you in a way that allows you to bless others from some of the profit, but it can't be handed over. Here, take this. Let's trade lives and I will live yours for a while and you can live mine and I'll suffer for your problems and you can have mine—which are so much less of a burden than yours!

If only we really could bring each other relief that way. When someone is having a hard life we could say, "I'll trade you for a week!"

But our life is the one thing we can't really and truly ever give away. We can sacrifice for others but we can't exchange souls like a house swap.

Today I am grateful for this: My husband's smile and how when I stood at the bathroom door this morning he suddenly turned and kissed me with shaving cream all over his face—and then mine.

A shaving cream kiss. This is a big thing. This is a gold nugget. This makes sense.

The Thirstiest Days
of Your Life

I recently received an email from a reader named Greta, who asked for advice on getting through those first early days of sobriety.

"I can't imagine *never* drinking again," she wrote.

If you've ever tried to put down an addiction, you can probably relate. Given how hard it is to abstain for even a day, the idea of doing so for the rest of your life borders on the absurd.

The good news is that we don't have to stay sober *forever*. We only have to stay sober one day—or even one hour or minute—at a time. When we resist the impulse to project our efforts into the future, we increase our chances for success today.

And here's more good news.

While anxiety, desperation, and misery are completely normal in early sobriety, these feelings are not at all indicative of life in recovery: *You won't always feel this way!* But let's face it. Reassurances like these mostly ring hollow when you're facing the thirstiest days of your life.

What Greta really wants to know, and maybe you do, too—is how *do* you make it through even a single day? How do you cope with cravings, anxiety, and the increasingly appealing idea of stopping some *other* day?

It's a huge subject, but here are some of the ideas that helped me most.

Meditate on Mantras.

At first, I was appalled by the dorky clichés I heard in meetings. Then I discovered that they *worked*. When you are trying to scale the steep rock face of temptation, these deceptively simple sayings are like footholds to keep you steady. Meditating on, "Let go and let God," or "The first drink will get you drunk," can save the day.

Refuse to Romance the Drink.

Your addict brain will trick you into remembering only the good parts of drinking—how sophisticated you felt, or how lovely it was to drink while cooking. Counter these visions by recalling—out loud if necessary—the less pretty truth about where drinking finally took you. There's nothing romantic about guzzling wine while locked in your bathroom or _____ (fill in the blank for you).

Get Sweet on Sweets.

Especially if you drank wine or sugary cocktails, sucking on a jolly rancher, sitting down for a flavored coffee in the afternoon, or falling in love with ice cream can help relieve your cravings. I'm not advocating trading addictions, but sugar can be a helpful tool if not overly abused. Besides, ask yourself how many calories you used to *drink* a day?

Remember H.A.L.T.

This acronym stands for four powerful triggers—Hungry, Angry, Lonely, Tired. Often, our urge to drink is being exacerbated by one of these conditions. In my early days, I was shocked to realize how often my desperation went away after I had eaten dinner or dealt with a resentment. Self-care is a HUGE key to success in early sobriety.

Drink Bubbles.

Many alcoholics in recovery still feel compelled to have a glass, bottle, or can in their hand at all times. Since water is one of the few beverages we can safely consume in such large quantities, a surprising number of us get hooked on sparkling water or club soda. Something about the bubbly texture or a hint of flavor makes it feel more special.

Stay Busy and Connected.

It goes without saying that you should attend as many recovery meetings as possible. But you also shouldn't sit around and let your mind wander. During my first sober summer, Dave and I took up biking and it helped tremendously. Revisit an old hobby or find a new one.

Rediscover Your Knees.

As you get out of bed in the morning, slide directly to your knees and ask God to keep you sober today. At night, kneel and thank God for keeping you sober today. If at any other point during the day you are seriously tempted to drink—your knees work then, too. "Help!" is a prayer God loves to answer.

Dedicate Your Relinquishments.

What I mean by this is, turn your choice to abstain into a sacrifice you make for God. This last tip only makes sense if you have a personal God, I admit. But if I had to choose one idea that helped me most, it might be this.

Early in my recovery, the sight of others enjoying drinking pained me—even if I pretended otherwise.

One afternoon, I found myself with Dave at a party where everyone was imbibing. Standing there with my iced tea, I wanted a glass of wine so deeply it hurt. Then something I'd read earlier that day by Gerald May came to mind. He'd written about how we can imbue our suffering with meaning and purpose by dedicating our relinquishments back to God.

At the time, it sounded like mumbo jumbo. But that afternoon, something clicked. What if I could *not* drink, "unto God?" What if I could view my choice to abstain as a sacrifice of love, instead of just suffering for nothing?

I shut my eyes and prayed a short prayer, dedicating my thirst and pain back to God. Almost immediately, my perspective shifted. I was no longer a deprived person at a party. I was participating in a spiritual practice.

The Hope of Change

To journey without being changed
is to be a nomad.
To change without journeying
is to be a chameleon.
To journey and to be transformed
by the journey
is to be a pilgrim.
—*Mark Nepo*

I often say in recovery meetings that if God took me out of his oven today and declared me "done"—I'd be utterly devastated. Which is probably why I love this poem by Mark Nepo.

Few things mean more to me these days than the hope of change—the promise that I might be a better person tomorrow than I am today.

This wasn't always the case. Especially during my drinking years, I was the nomad—journeying without being changed. How could it be otherwise? You can't numb yourself to life and expect to be shaped by your experiences. You can't pickle your brain in alcohol every day and hope to grow anything but *smaller*.

I have also been the second person in Nepo's poem—the chameleon who changes *without* journeying. Especially during the formative years of my Christian faith, what I fancied as spiritual growth—changing my beliefs, friends, and taboos—was really more about conforming to the Christian culture around me.

When I first got sober, I imagined that by removing alcohol from my system, I'd instantly be restored to some former, better Heather—and spiritual transformation would quickly follow. Instead, putting down the bottle did little or nothing to improve my personality. Mostly, it threw a spotlight on my immaturity and selfishness.

Given this painful blow to my ego, I determined to work a "strong program"—to be the best damn recovering drunk there ever was— much the same way I had once striven to be a "strong Christian." I was arrogant enough to think I could accomplish that without actually working the 12 Steps or getting a sponsor.

After six months, I relapsed. *Duh!*

In the five years since, I've slowly been learning the difference between the part I play in my spiritual growth and the part only God can play. I can take needed actions and make good choices. I can try to do the next right thing. But only God has the power to actually *transform* my soul, to alter my nature at its very core.

So if I want to become the pilgrim in Nepo's poem—*journeying and being changed by the journey*—my most important job is to offer the least possible resistance to the work.

For me, that means taking time every morning to sit in silence and surrender. It means inviting God to access every corner of my journey.

The First Punch

I meet a lot of people in recovery who are mad at God. In many cases, their anger can be traced to past hurtful experiences with religious people or institutions. Others carry a grudge because they can't reconcile a good God with the needless suffering, senseless evil, and unfixable poverty they see in the world. Still others blame God for wounds they suffered at the hands of other people.

When I talk with an alcoholic who resents God, I've found that it doesn't help much for me to defend or try to repair his reputation. More and more I am learning to ask, "Have you told God how you feel?"

It's surprising how many people haven't.

Ironically, many of us have been conditioned to treat God like he's not really there.

While attending church in my early twenties, I picked up on the idea that it was wrong to get angry at God, and even worse to let this truth slip—especially to his face. (*Watch out!*)

My pastor never actually said, "Don't be honest with God if you're mad at him." But it was understood: *God is to be treated with kid gloves. He is to be praised at all times.*

Which made sense to me. Except it didn't, really.

I mean, if God already knows my heart, why try to hide what's in it? And if God is so great, how can his ego be so fragile? I must have concluded that *pretending* is simply the price you pay if you are impossibly angry with the very Person whose love and help you need the most.

Around this same time, I was trying to cope with painful childhood wounds from my father and stepfather. I carried deep resentments toward all men—and secretly, toward God too. After all, God made men. And since in my mind God was singularly male, he was doubly guilty.

One winter afternoon, a painful event in my marriage triggered my outrage. But this time, instead of lashing out at my first husband, as was my habit, I let God have it.

For at least an hour, I beat God up for every bad thing a man had ever done to me. I screamed like a banshee in his face and pounded his chest with my fists. (Okay, it was the bed that got the pounding.) I accused him of heartlessness, perverseness, deafness, and impotence.

And I didn't apologize afterward.

Instead, I waited for God to strike me dead. Even hoped for it. Still crying, I told him that would be just fine by me. I was *that* mad.

After a while (perhaps when God thought it was safe), I felt a presence near me. And then I felt—in a way I can't explain or defend—that I was understood. That God welcomed my honest outpouring of grief and anger—and in some very real way even shared it.

Nothing has been the same between us since. Though plenty has gone wrong. In the years to come, I would greatly compromise my relationship with God in countless ways, and not just through alcohol. As it turns out, there are a thousand ways to betray God.

But there are a thousand *more* ways to make up with him.

In the meantime, God's invitation to be completely honest and real with him—to come exactly as I am, not as I wish I were—has never been withdrawn.

If you are angry at God today, are you willing to tell him why? What if God is inviting you to throw the first punch?

A Beautiful Day
to Hit Bottom

With the New Year upon us, I'm expecting to see some fresh, unfamiliar faces in my meetings. Recovery is kind of like an athletic club that way—come January, you get a big surge in membership.

Frankly, I can't wait. Nothing helps me more than to hear newbies fresh off their nightmares remind me of what I escaped.

But today I want to speak to the person who is still standing at the threshold. You know who you are. You know you have a problem, but you haven't yet found the courage to ask for help.

People who haven't been where you are right now can't possibly understand how scary this place is. You feel out of control, miserable, desperate. Yet you feel trapped. Your brain is burning up with questions: *Has my life come to this—really? What if people find out?*

And worse: *What if the help actually works, and I have to change?*

And worse yet: *What if it doesn't work, and I can't change?*

No wonder most addicts stand at the door of surrender for such a long time, unwilling to consider recovery until we hit some new, terrible "bottom"—a low so low that we become willing to do whatever it takes to get free.

It makes sense that we have to get in a lot of pain before we're ready to risk change. But there's a problem with putting too much stock in some distant or elusive "bottom." While we continue to spiral downward, waiting for things to get worse, *terrible things can happen.*

Duh, right? And yet, most addicts are genuinely shocked when we have a car accident, lose a career, or end up in jail. Had we really seen the catastrophe coming, we'd have gotten off the elevator a few floors up.

Hiding in this truth is good news about bottoms that's easy to miss. Even if we've lost the power of choice over our addiction, we still have the power of choice over our decision to reach for help. In recovery we often remind each other, "You can exit the elevator at any time. Your 'bottom' is where you decide to get off."

When I first came to meetings and heard all the horror stories, I remember thinking, *What the heck? My bottom wasn't that bad. I could have drunk for ten more years!*

That was my addiction speaking, of course. It's a twisted kind of logic that kills many good people every day.

A more truthful revelation came to me later: *I could have come into recovery years ago and spared myself and those I love so much heartache!*

Unfortunately, many of us have to get sober in order to discover that we *want* to be sober. Crazy, huh? But until we experience the miracle of recovery, we can't imagine how it could be anything less than miserable. We assume that we'll be the exact same person—minus the comfort of our drug of choice.

And if all we do is stop, it's a pretty accurate prediction.

But it doesn't have to be that way, I promise. In recovery, we learn that we don't just need to say *no* to our addiction, we *get* to say *yes* to God—and to a whole new way of life.

I know that sounds scary. Overwhelming, even. But on the other side of that threshold lies the opportunity for a new kind of happiness you can't even imagine now.

The first step is simply to take the first step.

What are you waiting for?

Today is a beautiful day to hit bottom.

Belly Button Grace

I ran across another gem by author and poet, Mark Nepo:

"Each person is born with an unencumbered spot—free of expectation and regret, free of ambition and embarrassment, free of fear and worry—an umbilical spot of grace where we were each first touched by God."

Wait a minute, I thought. *He's talking about my spiritual belly button!*

And he's not even being a little bit silly. His words remind me that as surely as my mother gave birth to my body, God gave birth to my soul. I was made by Love, in love, for love. And a sacred place in the center of my being is permanently marked by the memory of this making.

For me, this center is where I connect to my truest, most authentic self. And when I live from this place, I find freedom from the tyranny of my ego.

To be honest, some days, this knowledge—that I really am born of God and some remnant of his perfect divine spark still lives in me—is the only part of my life that makes sense.

The same morning I read about my spiritual belly button, I also ran across this line from Brennan Manning: "God's love is based on nothing, and this is where we find our security."

If "based on nothing" leaves you feeling anything but secure, consider this: *Because God's love for us isn't based on anything, nothing can shake it.*

Taken together, the two quotes suggest a way to think about God's love that goes way beyond the human version we so often project onto him. For example, we tend to think of love as a feeling we have in response to another person. But feelings can be fragile and fleeting, so we easily get insecure.

How many of us have ever said to a spouse or lover: "But *why* do you love me? Tell me all the reasons." And the person will try. They'll list some of our finer qualities and more endearing quirks.

But to God, love needs no "whys," because it is Who he is. If God could find in me even one reason *to* love me, it would be devastating, since it would mean that with a little more thought on his part, or a little worse day on mine, he could find a reason *not* to.

More and more, when I don't feel God's love, I'm learning not to ask him to remind me of all the ways I'm special (which only appeals to my ego anyway). Instead, I make time to sit in silence with him, naked in my soul as the day I was born, with nothing to say and nothing to give and nothing to show and nothing to prove my worth.

Only then does some deep part of me understand that I can't do anything to make God love me more or less. In that moment, I manage to touch that umbilical spot of grace that marks the truth of Whose I am.

And it saves me.

Hum Loud, Blow Hard

I picked up my friend, Hafiz. And I remembered again the reason I love his poems. Here's an excerpt from the one I read:

"Restlessness and a lack of peace
can play a vital part in your inner unfoldment.
If you ever become too complacent, too
accepting of your sorrow or shadow self,
the moon might fling a beehive into your
undies and that should wake you up."

That woke me up, for sure. And it made me realize that God was awake, too—and he was laughing. Me with my sleep-smashed hair hoping for spiritual revelation and getting bees in my underwear.

It reminded me of what happened last Monday when I drove with a friend in her car to a luncheon in Denver to hear author William Cope Moyers speak on addiction.

He was great, I'm sure. But his wasn't the lesson I remember. My friend, you see, recently got one of those new-fangled breathalyzers installed in her car, courtesy of the legal system. Every twenty minutes or so, this gadget would start to beep and she'd rush to pick it up so she could hum really loud and blow really hard into the mouth piece for about ten seconds—to prove she hasn't been drinking alcohol.

The challenge for her, especially with me in the car, was to make it through without laughing.

Amazingly, she doesn't resent the device at all. "It's great for my ego," she admitted. "I'm driving along and just as I'm thinking too much or taking life too seriously—it beeps and I get to feel ridiculous."

Aha, you see?

Profound advice arrives, even without the waterfall of God's love. Just . . . Hum loud. Blow hard. Repeat.

How To Fall Out of Hate with Yourself

ran across an old TV clip from *Two and a Half Men,* back when Charlie Sheen still starred:

> The character Jake is kneeling at the toilet, throwing up after drinking.
>
> Charlie says, "You know, your body is sending you a message . . . that alcohol is poison."
>
> "Then why do *you* drink?" counters Jake.
>
> "Because," says Charlie, "I have things inside of me that I need to kill."

Isn't it amazing how profound truth can creep into something so banal as a TV sit-com?

Technically, alcohol *is* poison, which is why you can die from over-drinking. But I was even more struck by Charlie's explanation for why we pursue self-destructive compulsions: "I have things inside of me that I need to kill."

It's one of the great paradoxes of addiction. On the one hand, it's characterized by the pursuit of pleasure at any cost, and it reeks of self-love.

On the other hand, every binge, hit, or burger bender proves nothing so much as that we hate—and want to hurt—some part of ourselves.

During my drinking days, I didn't understand this. I knew that I hated myself *because of* the things alcohol made me do. But I couldn't see how my drinking itself was a manifestation of the very self-loathing I drank to drown.

For years, I starred in my own sit-com rerun, except it wasn't funny: *See Heather hate herself. See Heather drink to feel better. See Heather hate herself even more...*

How did I ever escape the vicious cycle?

I recently revisited this question when a desperate alcoholic pleaded with me in an email: "Heather, if you have the ANSWER, please share it!"

For a second there I actually racked my brain. Like there was a simple solution I forgot to mention.

But all I have is my story. All I know is that one ordinary morning, hung-over and horrified by what my life had become, I fell sobbing to my knees by my bed and made my full surrender, something I'd genuinely tried—and failed—to do so many times before.

So what got me across the line this time? In some ways, it's a still a mystery to me. But here's what I know for sure.

It wasn't my enormous self-hate; if anything, it was an experience of God's overwhelming love in the face of my shame.

We often remind each other in Christian circles, "It's God's kindness that leads us to repentance." But I'm not sure we really believe that it's true. Instead, so many of us try to hate ourselves sober—only to experience the talons of addiction digging deeper into our souls.

If you're one of those people who feels stuck in an endless cycle of trying harder and praying longer and repenting until you're blue in the face—only to fall on your face again . . . you might try this. Instead of struggling to let go of your substance, see if you can't let go of self-loathing.

If you can, get on your knees by your bed. And then in your mind crawl across those sharp rocks of shame to where a waterfall of God's mercy thunders down without reason or measure, and put your head under it until nothing else makes sense.

Cry out for help like a person dying—because maybe you finally are.

Maybe *this* is what it takes to kill what you hate—not more hate, but an encounter with Love so great that you can't receive it without letting go of everything else, including your life, your will, your way.

When you finally get up off your knees, let God wrap you in a towel and be quiet with him for a while.

Then go to a recovery meeting. Or check into treatment. Or tell a friend.

In a very real sense, your life has just begun.

If you're one of those fortunate folks who is already in recovery, I have some something to say to you, too.

Self-hate can't *keep* you sober any more than it can get you there. And nothing will drag you back into the ditch of addiction faster than listening to the voice that says you can't change, you're not doing it right, and you don't deserve to be sober.

Resist that voice, friend. Find the waterfall again. And let God's *kindness* lead you forward on the path of grace.

What's God Gonna Make Me Do?

Last week I got an email from a reader who asked for prayer because she is trying to do something really "scary."

I expected her to go on to say she was moving to a Third World country or going to have to speak in public. But what had her so scared was a recent decision to "surrender to God's will."

I so get this.

Somewhere along the way, I too picked up the idea that the only thing scarier than missing God's will for my life was signing up for it. The logic of my fear went something like this: Since trials and hardship bring spiritual growth . . . and since God's main concern is not our happiness, but our holiness . . . surely, his will for me is bound to bring misery, right?

Not long ago, I was in a recovery meeting when a woman I admire told us, "When I'm not sure what to do, I do whatever is hardest or will hurt the most, since that's probably God's will for me." I didn't know whether to admire her more—or run screaming from the room.

Of course, God *does* allow us to suffer pain and he does use it to help us grow. And yes, the right choice is often a difficult one. But that doesn't mean *all* suffering comes by God's hand, or that his plans for our good *always* have to hurt.

Thankfully, I no longer believe that God doesn't care about my happiness, or that he is so intent on my spiritual progress that he is bent on taking me down the most difficult path possible. I think it's just the *opposite*. If God is a perfect, loving Father, it has to be.

Think about how we are with our own kids. Sure, we allow them to learn hard lessons and suffer consequences so they'll grow up to be people who love God and others. But if given half a chance, we'd also follow them around all day trying to ensure their landings were soft and their sufferings minimized.

I think God is like that with us.

And if you ask me, the same logic applies to the idea of *knowing* God's will for my life.

Back in the day, I didn't think so. I thought God's plan for me was a huge mystery that I had to solve—or else. If God was feeling generous, he might leave a few breadcrumbs on my path. But if I missed these signs and took a wrong turn, it was all my fault, and I might be stuck in God's plan B—or even Z—forever!

Of course, God is not like that. Would you watch your own child taking a wrong turn and wait for her to get lost in order to make your point that she should pay closer attention?

When I first got into recovery, I was surprised at the ease with which most of these folks—many of whom had no religious background—spoke about God's will. They didn't seem to fear it, nor did they seem greatly mystified by it, either.

By their example, I came to understand the logic of love. I learned that I could trust God to guide me gently, without tricks or traps. And I learned that God's will for me happens naturally as I surrender my own will to him. I don't have to search high and low. I don't have to be afraid of where God will take me next. I only have to do the next right thing he's placed in my path.

The Bone, the Pebble, and *that* Person

Years ago on the TV show, *Grey's Anatomy*, Meredith famously said to her friend Christina, "You're my person..." We understood that she meant, "You're the one person on the planet I entirely trust with my secrets and problems."

Viewers resonated so much with this phrase that, "You're my *person*," became part of our vernacular.

Sorry, but this is not about *this* person, but his or her opposite. I'm talking about *that* person—the co-worker, friend, acquaintance, or relative—who endlessly annoys you, competes with you, is passive-aggressive, exhausting, dismissive, insensitive, or seems intent on making you look or feel bad.

The other night I went to a recovery meeting where this was the topic. I heard so many smart things, but it was surprisingly heartbreaking, too. Regardless of how long we've been sober or how much we love God, so many of us have struggled, or are now struggling painfully, with That Person.

I once spent *years* chewing a bone with one guy's name on it. Night after night, I asked Dave to gnaw alongside me, and sometimes he did. The person never changed one iota and we both got cracked teeth.

Part of what makes That Person so problematic is that they're not going away any time soon. Unlike those folks in our past who we could forgive and happily forget—your anti-person is like a permanent pebble in your shoe.

The problem is quite simple: How can you not live in a constant state of resentment?

Since it's highly unlikely That Person will change, our hope lies in changing our response. It's almost like we have to develop a posture of *pre-forgiveness*, or *forgiveness preparedness*.

I think what I'm describing is an ongoing spiritual process that isn't even *supposed* to be easy. But drawing on the shared wisdom of my fellow alcoholics, here are some admittedly hard questions we can ask ourselves that just might give us a jump-start:

What is my part? When people are problematic to us, it feels like they *are* the problem. But we always have a part, no matter how obscure. How do I think and talk about this person to others? How do I interact with him or her, and what kind of energy do I put out? Am I participating in a subtle but toxic dynamic that takes two to sustain?

Is my pride in the way? Nine times in ten, That Person offends my *ego*, my sense of importance, or my pride. How could greater humility on my part change the dynamics for *me*? A person can't hurt my pride if I've already set it aside— which can feel impossible, at times. But just being *aware* of my ego is a good place to start.

Is the person I'm bugged at just like me? I've heard it said in meetings, "You can spot it because you've got it." Often, a person's attitudes or actions annoy us precisely because we see the same faults in ourselves . . . *and we hate them.* Practicing self-compassion can radically change how we react to these unattractive qualities in others.

Am I being dishonest with my expectations? Sometimes we have expectations of people that aren't in line with what this person has already taught us is true about them. It's unfair to be shocked and dismayed when That Person behaves exactly like I knew he or she would.

Is my own pretense part of the problem? It can be tempting to pretend to That Person that everything is great. But love doesn't ask us to participate in an ongoing lie—or to be

doormats. When I put up with a pattern of behavior, I participate in it and appear to accept it. Why not make sure the person doesn't care enough to change?

Could this pebble in my shoe have a greater purpose? Ultimately, it's up to me whether this person makes my life miserable or becomes a gift to help me grow in compassion and tolerance. We don't learn those qualities around people we love and agree with. It's in the hard, daily work of softening toward someone difficult that we grow and are changed.

Could radical generosity change my heart? In recovery we pray for the people we resent and ask God to bless them with everything we would want for ourselves. And it helps! Something inside of us shifts as we view the person through God's eyes. Another idea is to give That Person the very thing—for example, praise, money, or loyalty—that we most want to withhold. Something about being generous breaks the bonds of our resistance.

So how about you? Do you have That Person in your life right now? Or maybe two? How do *you* cope, and what questions would you add to this list?

If you've got no bone to chew, and there's no pebble in your shoe today, step lightly and rejoice.

"It's Going to Be Okay"

I picture her about two inches tall, sometimes smaller. She lives inside my chest, but she has freedom to travel into my brain and maybe even into my ear canals. Sometimes, she slides down into my stomach and I know she's there because I can feel her kicking the walls. She is always upset, you see. She exists in a state of perpetual panic, her hair on fire, her arms waving wildly, her voice shrill as she yells at me to do something more to fix the situation.

The situation varies.

During the light of day, fully conscious, I can handle her pretty well. Sometimes I impress myself when I drown out her cries with the gentle voice of reason. I reframe the situation. I use my spiritual tools. I achieve something close to calm.

But in the wee hours of night, I am defenseless—and she knows it. Half-awake, her logic makes sense to my mushy brain. At 3 a.m., she is not hysterical, she is undeniably *right*.

The sky is falling! And I'm lying here doing nothing to stop it. How can I think of sleeping when I should be hard at work worrying? After I've let her talk me into a tizzy, I usually remember God. I try to pray, but then she chimes in and I can't tell her voice from mine and I sound ridiculous in my own ears.

This morning, I lost my temper. I shouted in her face, *What can I do to shut you up?*

Get drunk, she said, with a wicked smile.

I should have seen that coming, but it felt like a slap in the face. I reminded her that the sky is supposedly falling and could crash around our ears at any moment. *Will a drink make it better?* She smirked like I used to at six.

We might still be talking, she and I, except my husband turned over and curled into my back and I felt him awake and I knew that soon he would get up to make coffee.

A dim light began to fill our bedroom. A few birds started to tweet. There would be no getting back to sleep. Before I swung myself out of bed, I told her what I always do on mornings like these, when I'm exhausted before I even rise.

"It's going to be okay," I said, and I know it's not a lie.

Because I will not drink today.

Snow in My Coffee

Saturday morning, I got snow in my coffee.

As I walked my dog down the alley, his red leash in one hand, caffeine in the other, several dandruff-like flakes floated gently into my cup. It was that kind of snow that is barely there, dry and flyaway. The kind where each unhurried flake bops about on its own current of air and doesn't seem to care if it ever touches ground.

I want to live that way. Effortless and breezy, not trying too hard, never mind if I don't get there . . . so long as I land in God's cup.

That sounds so simple, doesn't it? As we like to say in recovery, *Easy does it.*

But in my experience, few things in life are *harder* than taking it easy. Which was a huge part of alcohol's appeal to me back in the day, by the way. Getting drunk was as close as I could come to relaxing, and it seemed the only way to drown out the voice of my ego yelling, *Go faster! Try harder! You have to win!*

This past weekend, my husband Dave flew to visit our grown kids. I stayed behind, in large part hoping to make hay on some projects. Instead, I got sick—*again!* I couldn't believe it. How could God let this happen when I'm already so overwhelmed? I've been pleading with him for weeks, "If you don't do something soon to help me manage all this, some very important things are going to fall off the table!"

But on my walk that day, as I watched those snowflakes drop into my coffee, I finally understood.

I'm not supposed to succeed at managing it all—even with God's help. I'm supposed to let a few things fall, and then trust God to catch them.

How to Drink with a Recovering Alcoholic

et's say that Dave and I are meeting you and a few others for dinner at a restaurant with a great wine list. You know that I'm a recovering alcoholic, but you're accustomed to having a glass with dinner. The waiter approaches the table and makes much ado about a new Cabernet on their list. Then he asks, "Can I start you off with something to drink?"

I'm setting up this scenario to think through with you how to be more at ease socially around folks in recovery. I know it can get awkward—not quite like what you feel around a friend who just went through a devastating loss, but close. So how should you respond?

You could pass on wine and order water for my sake. You could wait and see what Dave does, then follow suit. You could ask if I mind if you drink. Or you could simply order the Cabernet without asking. Most people I've talked to would opt to pass on drinking, or feel bad if they don't. What about you?

Here's my take on our dinner together: If I thought you abstained from drinking to protect me from temptation, I'd appreciate your intention. But I'd also feel needlessly coddled.

A lot of my friends in recovery would feel the same way. Of course, we know that people mean well. Thoughtfulness and sensitivity are never wrong. So when someone is overly cautious around me—apologizing profusely, say, because they mentioned a margarita—I laugh and let them off the hook. Because you know what? There is no hook.

That said, though, I've been thinking lately that some of the awkwardness non-recovery folks experience around us might be traced back to a few understandable but inaccurate assumptions about how recovery actually works.

For example:

People think we stay sober by resisting the temptation to drink. If this was the case, few of us could achieve long-term sobriety. Instead, God eventually lifts from us our obsession to drink. We are given a daily reprieve from cravings and compulsions so long as we tend to our spiritual progress.

People assume we can't be around those who are drinking socially. While no sober person wants to hang out with a bunch of people who are blotto, most alcoholics are comfortable at social gatherings where others are imbibing responsibly. Some of us discover we have *more* fun sober at parties than we ever did drinking.

People think we are against alcohol and would love to see it banned. Sure, we hate the damage that drugs and alcohol bring to our world. But we understand that normal drinkers have every right to enjoy alcohol, just as people without an allergy to peanuts have every right to eat them. The miracle of recovery is that it *transforms our relationship with alcohol.* Here's how our literature explains what it feels like to enjoy healthy recovery:

"We are not fighting it [alcohol], neither are we avoiding temptation. We feel as though we had been placed in a position of neutrality—safe and protected. The problem has been removed. It does not exist for us. That is how we react so long as we keep in fit spiritual condition."

One qualifier: Probably nothing I've said here applies to a newly sober alcoholic. I know from personal experience that those early days of learning to do life sober come with unique challenges. If you're unsure in a social situation where a person is on his or her journey, I say go ahead and risk a brief bout of awkward. Ask as privately as you can what kind of response on your part would be most helpful. At least the person will know you care.

I do my best to try to alleviate potential elephant-in-the-room moments in advance. Something simple and direct is good: "I won't be drinking tonight, but I really hope you'll feel free." Or, earlier in my sobriety, I might have asked, "Do you mind if we stick to iced tea?"

These days, if Dave and I are meeting up with people who know my story, I text or email in advance: "By the way, I hope you'll feel free to imbibe tonight. Dave probably will, too—and I really don't mind."

I think I speak for most of my friends who have been in recovery for a while when I say we prefer to be at a table where everyone is enjoying themselves.

Just don't look too surprised when we propose a toast with a glass of fine water.

"Me Too"

Not long ago my husband Dave came home from meeting with a friend who is going through an unwanted divorce and is in a lot of pain.

"You know," he remarked. "It's amazing how it works. I'm sitting across from this guy realizing that none of my successes in life are of any use to him. It's only my failures that are helpful."

That's so true, isn't it? Our personal achievements, though wonderful to us, are rarely all that valuable to hurting people. Instead, it's our past mistakes and brokenness that bring the most hope to others. If God brought us through, maybe they can make it, too.

I forget this so easily. A couple hours before an interview this week, I stared out my hotel window, gulping back fear, trying to sense God's reassurance. I kept waiting for him to say, "You're going to do so great!"

But instead, he reminded me that I'm not there to impress or perform, but simply to say to some folks out there, "Me too." *Look at me. I'm just like you, and I too found myself in a place of desperation that I never imagined possible. I too, spiraled into addiction despite being a Christian. I too, couldn't seem to fix or change myself. And yet here I am today. . . .*

Author and fellow recovering alcoholic Brennan Manning wrote,

"One of the most healing words I ever spoke as a confessor was to an old priest with a drinking problem.

'Just a few years ago,' I said, 'I was a hopeless alcoholic in the gutter in Fort Lauderdale.'

'You?' he cried, 'O thank God!'"

This reminds me of when I met Susan. I was still in the depths of my drinking and Susan was marrying one of Dave's best friends.

When she eventually admitted that she was an alcoholic in recovery, my first reaction was to cringe: *How embarrassing for her!*

And yet, in some secret place deep inside of me, her confession lit a spark of hope. If she could be happy in recovery, maybe I could too. Of course, Susan had no idea how God was using her in my life.

So maybe, "Me too" isn't just something we get to say, but a posture of vulnerability we get to live every day.

I think about Jesus enduring suffering and humiliation. He had to face every temptation known to man, be rejected, reviled, and betrayed by a beloved friend.

Maybe Jesus was God's way of saying, "Me too."

The Problem with God's Power

During an interview when my memoir *Sober Mercies* released, the host seemed surprised to learn that I was a Christian *before* I spiraled into alcoholism. "How did that happen?" he asked.

I wanted to answer, "One drink at a time."

But I understood the question behind his question: If I rely on God's power to keep me sober today, why couldn't that same power have prevented my becoming an alcoholic in the first place?

My honest answer is: I think it could have. God's help and strength were always available to me. But instead of relying on God's power, I was determined to beat my drinking problem on my own terms.

Which begs the question: Why did I continue on a path of self-reliance even though it was so obviously failing me?

It's one of the great mysteries of addiction, for sure. But here's what I think was true for me: I chose to rely on own measly power for the simple reason that it allowed me to stay in charge and feel in control.

The "problem" with God's power is that it comes to us by way of surrender. He empowers us to do *his* will, not ours. We can say all day long that we rely on God, but if we're still intent on running the show, the power we're trusting is our own.

It's really that simple. And it's really that hard.

When I was little, my mother used to break a lot of hairbrushes on my bottom while I smiled and told her the spankings didn't hurt. It was my way of letting her know that I still wasn't beat.

My younger brother, Jim, handled spankings differently. He ran for his life. With our mother in hot pursuit, he'd race through the house crying, "How many swats? How many swats?"

Mom would yell out a number, threatening more if he didn't stop.

Jim would wail in protest, and run even faster. The number of swats continued to climb until she finally caught him.

I'd watch and laugh. What an idiot! Didn't he realize he was just making it worse?

But I think I was a lot like Jim when it came to my fear of trusting God with my alcoholism. God wasn't chasing me around with a hair brush, mind you. But I was too intent on running to turn around and give up.

On the other hand, some of us addicts resist surrender more like I used to submit to spankings. We go through the motions of attending meetings and taking the steps. But inside, we're still unwilling to capitulate or give up control to God. What looks like surrender is simply compliance, and it will only take us so far.

It was one morning six years ago this April when I finally abandoned myself to God. My running days were over.

But I've found that one surrender—no matter how sincere—is not enough. Every day, I have to choose God's will and God's way all over again.

The Power of a Pause

Dave and I got to go to Oregon to see my son Nathan and his wife Kelsey in their first home. We had a marvelous time walking by the river near their house, talking over yummy dinners, and lounging around while Kelsey worked on graduate-level calculus.

As usual, visiting Central Oregon took me back in time. Something about the air, the smell of pinecones, the cold by the river, evoked a deep memory of feeling desperate for a drink.

It also reminded me that I have to work hard around family not to slip into an old, familiar, brattier version of myself. The one, for example, who thinks she's so damn funny and values a joke over someone else's feelings.

Maybe you can relate. It seems no matter how old you grow or how much you like to think you've changed, when you get around family or friends who are intimately familiar with an earlier version of you, it's easy to slip into old patterns of behavior.

I was in a recovery meeting once when a guy who was reading from our literature accidentally substituted the phrase *character defaults* for *character defects*. We all agreed that it was a helpful, maybe even divine, mistake.

Some of us aren't fond of the word *defect*—or worse, *defective*—since it seems to describe something unfixable. Talking about our *defaults* seems a kinder, and maybe even a more accurate, way to discuss our shortcomings.

In Step 7 of the recovery process, we ask God to remove these from us. But first, we spend the entire Step 6 becoming *willing* to have them removed. Early on, this didn't make sense to me. Why would a person *not* want God to remove their flaws?

Viewing them as defaults—what we do automatically if nothing prevents us—makes the answer easier to understand. Most of our defaults began in childhood as coping mechanisms that worked for us. Now that we're grown, they no longer serve much good purpose. More often than not, they may even work *against* us. But we still revert to them because they're just so damn familiar.

For example, as a kid I relied on sarcasm, rudeness, and humor at others' expense as a way to shield myself from vulnerability or hurt. I don't like it when I act this way. (Others don't much either.) And yet I struggle to surrender a way of being that comes so naturally to me.

Plus, it's kind of fun to act like a brat.

Clearly, this is where the willingness part comes into it.

But here's the rub. I've found that willingness and asking God for help aren't quite enough, especially when I'm in a situation that triggers my defaults. What really helps, and what helped this weekend, is another important tool of recovery.

It's just one little word. And it seems so small. But when practiced on purpose it has the power to stop a freight train of character defaults in their tracks.

I'm talking about the great and mighty … pause. That small space of time in which you interrupt the natural flow of your inclinations long enough to remind yourself who you are now and who you want you to be. Long enough to think about the other person (or persons).

A pause is your opportunity to invite God to help you *respond* instead of *react*.

A pause is your chance to ask, what is the opposite of my natural impulse here?

I don't mean to make it sound easy. Pausing to change course can feel unnatural, even wrong. Like trying to row upstream. But it works. Sure, I let go a few jokes on Saturday night about how truly manly men like Nathan (not like Dave) don't mind if their wife points out a parking spot. I think I also zipped my lips in time to prevent a couple zingers, though.

Take it from me. A pause when you're feeling especially witty, in the spotlight, agitated, confused, tempted, or just silly might change your day. Or weekend.

Pause often enough, it might change the course of your life.

Call it Grace, Whatever, Something

The Worm's Waking

This is how a human being can change. There is a worm addicted to eating grape leaves. Suddenly, he wakes up, call it grace, whatever, something wakes him, and he is no longer a worm. He is the entire vineyard, and the orchard too, the fruit, the trunks, a growing wisdom and joy that does not need to devour. —*Rumi*

At the risk of ruining a little poem that lacks nothing, can I comment? I love the bold promise of Rumi's opening line: *This is how a human being can change.* As if!

As if the answer to this impossible problem could be tucked safely inside a few silly lines.

But maybe it can. I was that worm, once. I know what it means to be addicted to grapes, if not to the leaves. I know how it feels to let years pass you by while all you can do is drink and devour, and it is never enough.

And then one day, something changes. You wake up. The poet calls it *Grace* or *Whatever* or *Something*.

I am so often asked, "What happened? What changed? What was the turning point?" And I fumble for an answer. I mention the misery. How terrible it got. How dark. The blackouts. The awful mornings.

But maybe I should just say, *I woke up.* Or maybe, closer for me, *I remembered who I was.*

It was a little like that. I had a single moment, you see—a few weeks before the big breakdown. I was kneeling at the fireplace frantically trying to burn an empty liquor box before Dave came home from work and caught me. And out of nowhere, I saw myself. A woman made desperate by devouring. *What was I doing? Why was I pretending to be a secret drunk when I have always known that I was God's beloved?* It made no sense. *Why would I imagine I might need more when I am already one with Abundance? Why do I still?*

May I wake up again, and again tomorrow. And if you see me nodding off, shout *Something* or *Whatever* or *Grace* in my ear.

Why Just Say No is Just Not Enough

M y kids grew up in the era of Just Say No. Despite being mired in my own secret battle with alcoholism—or maybe because of it—I was desperate to protect my children from drugs and alcohol. My strategy with my kids involved:

- Discussions about the dangers of drug and alcohol use.
- Clear consequences for violating the no drugs or alcohol rule.
- Monitoring my kids' activities and friends.
- Watching for tell-tale signs of inebriation or drug use.
- Scare tactics. "Look at this article. Six teens were killed. That could be you!"

If home drug tests had been available then, I would have added that to the list. None of these tactics are wrong-headed, and most of them are helpful. But alone, they weren't enough to keep my kids from using drugs and alcohol as teens. My oldest son continued to battle substance abuse into his mid-twenties.

Today my approach as a parent would be radically different. Yes, we need to help our kids understand the dangers and give them moral and legal imperatives to abstain. But limiting our message to a Just Say No campaign ignores what I believe is the real problem: Drugs work.

Kids drink or get high for the same reasons adults do, after all. It helps them relax in social settings. It brings pleasure and even feelings of euphoria. It relieves performance anxiety. It gives them liquid courage to do hard things, like talk to the opposite sex. It helps them fit in, because most everyone else is partaking. It serves as an escape from the depression and disillusionment that are so much a part of high school. It eases isolation and loneliness. It puts them in touch with what feels like spiritual enlightenment—a mysterious connection to a larger reality.

And our mighty answer as a mom or dad to all that is, "Practice your 'no' honey"?

When you consider all the things a drug or drink can do for you and all the torturous questions adolescents are asking—*Who am I? Who loves me? What will become of me?*—why wouldn't kids want to indulge?

I can't tell you how many times I've heard people in recovery talk about the "magic" of their first experiences with alcohol or drugs. They say thing like, "I felt okay for the first time in my life," or "I had finally stumbled upon a way to escape what was going on inside."

Of course, the truth is that in the long run, and in anything but careful moderation in safe contexts, drugs and drink don't work. They stop doing all those promising things that lured you in the first place. They leave you with less than you had. They viciously turn on you. But I think it's grossly shortsighted and disrespectful of our kids' actual experience in the world to only acknowledge the dangers without also acknowledging the appeal.

Without that honesty, we're kidding ourselves to expect our kids to avoid a trap that has lured millions of smart adults to their deaths. Too often, it works like this: A kid grows up hearing how horrible and wrong it is to drink or drug, and then one day after a football game, he tries a joint or a couple of beers. Just as a pleasant buzz descends, a thought comes: *Mom and Dad lied. This is no big deal—and it feels good!*

Later, when he gets caught, parents pile on shame in hopes that the child's suffering will dissuade him from repeating the mistake. But here's what you have to understand. In his mind, the two don't correlate.

Mom's angry reactions and hysterics and alarm seem unrelated to the wonderful high he felt when he just said yes. Worse, piling on shame and guilt can actually launch kids more quickly into a cycle of substance abuse as they reach for relief from the pain of being such a disappointment to everyone.

Okay, so I've talked about why Just Say No is not enough, which is definitely not enough. In the next piece, I'll tell you what I think might work better, so please stay tuned.

Just Say Yes

Previously, I talked about why a Just Say No approach might not be enough when it comes to preventing substance abuse with our kids. I promised to tell you what I'd do differently.

Ever since, I've been wrestling with what to say. *What was I thinking? What do I know?*

Then came Saturday, and news of the tragic suicide of pastor Rick Warren's 27-year-old son, who apparently suffered from mental illness and depression. Such a sad and senseless loss—a bright kid, a loving and involved family, and still, a fatal choice.

As a person familiar with depression and suicide, it hit way too close to home. And it was a heartbreaking reminder that when it comes to complex issues like mental illness or substance abuse, none of us has a silver bullet. Not even the best parents—Christians included—can claim to have The Answer.

In the spirit of not having The Answer, I decided to scrap for now my list of 7 things you could do to protect your children from drug or alcohol abuse. Instead of advice, I want to share with you a few of my biggest regrets in hopes that you can glean from my mistakes.

I regret that I didn't listen well to my kids. I regret that I was too wrapped up in my own "important" grown up problems to take seriously enough just how deadly serious every single one of their problems seemed to them. I gave them answers. I wish I had given them my full attention.

I regret that I didn't show my kids more compassion. I can still picture my oldest son at 16, in bed in the middle of the day, his covers over his head. And there I was yelling at the top of my lungs about how could he do such a stupid thing. How mortified I was. How much he had let down and embarrassed his band mates and his very favorite teacher.

He'd been caught, you see, smoking dope and getting drunk while at the state competition for the prestigious jazz ensemble he was part of in high school. Police arrested him behind a McDonald's, and the school was forced to forfeit a contest they'd been favored to win.

Why didn't I hug him? Cry with him? Why didn't I get on my knees by his bed and talk to him about shame and guilt and assure him that he would find a way to make things right again and be forgiven—even though he couldn't change what happened?

Why didn't I ever, before or after that, talk to him about that nagging feeling of emptiness that we all feel no matter how much we love God or life? Why didn't I acknowledge how hard it is to turn down *the chance to feel better*? Why didn't I try to help him name and process the feelings he was so desperate to escape?

I regret that my words—don't drink or drug—were just too damn convenient. And what's worse, my words didn't at all match the real message I was sending by example. Which was, "Alcohol is the best way to unwind or reward yourself. No dinner, party, or celebration is complete without drinking. It's normal to rely on alcohol to navigate social situations. Drinking makes any bad thing better and any good thing great."

Obviously, how we approach our own compulsions—whether we numb through substances, food, endless TV, or even shopping—speaks louder to our kids than anything we say.

Then there's the role of heredity. I regret that I was too prideful to put Heather and her Dad and Grandmother together. Duh! We have a genetic predisposition to alcoholism in my family. Oh I could joke about it, sure. But I couldn't apply it to me or my kids until I was ready to stop drinking. And I wasn't, even for them.

What I don't regret at all is that today I'm living proof that when all my best efforts fail, God doesn't. He is always good. He has been my redeemer, and he will be my children's too.

Unfortunately, we can't require as a condition of trusting God that he will keep our kids safe from drugs or alcohol or any other harmful choice. But we can trust him to keep them safe in his eternal love in a way that goes way beyond this world.

Meantime, we parents get to lead the way in showing our kids how to Just Say Yes to life.

What Feelings Are For

Just Say No is just not enough. Not when it comes to our kids and drug abuse. I promised to tell you what I thought would work better—and then I sort of defaulted.

The problem was simple. Every point of advice I came up with either sounded too much like the basics of good parenting or seemed unrealistic to implement.

Lately, I've realized that if I could give just a single piece of advice to parents of teens it would be this: *See if you can wake them up.*

What I mean is most of us sleepwalk through our lives in reaction mode. Convinced that our thoughts are true and our emotions inevitable, we operate like this: We have a thought, it evokes a feeling, and we act accordingly.

Put another way, most of us live unconsciously. We don't step back and process our emotions on purpose, particularly those that we don't like. Instead, we try to change or escape them by the quickest means possible, which is a set up for using drugs, alcohol, or other mood-altering activities.

No wonder we have an epidemic of addiction in our society. And teens are especially vulnerable. Who experiences a greater storm of confusing or unwanted emotions than hormone-charged adolescents?

A joint or a six pack offers welcome relief and flashes of peace—at least at first. But what we all seem to forget is that feelings we refuse to feel don't actually go away. They gather at our backs and invisibly drive our choices in ways we don't understand.

No wonder feelings are the topic of so many recovery meetings. For the newly sober, raw emotions tend to come as a shock.

Personally, I felt like the Grand Canyon had opened up inside my chest, magnifying every feeling. *No wonder I drank!* I thought. *Un-muffled reality sucks!*

Of course, I eventually learned that embracing my feelings, staying present, and experiencing reality—getting to feel joy, as well as pain—was a much richer way to live. In one sense, it's the *only* way to live if you want to stay awake and be truly alive.

Which begs the question: Why do we wait for people to become addicts who need recovery before we teach them how to identify, honor, and work through—instead of around—their feelings?

If my own grown kids were teens now, I'd work hard to teach them this priceless skill. *Your thoughts are not you,* I'd tell them. *Neither are your feelings. You are* having *them, which means you have choices.*

Since thinking leads to feeling, I'd show my kids how to step back, notice a train of thought, and ask if it's true or helpful. If it's neither, we'd talk about how to reframe the situation in their mind.

Same with feelings. *What are your feelings trying to tell you?* I'd ask. Then we'd talk about how to honor your feelings without letting them *be* you...and run your life into the ditch.

If all that sounds too complicated or woo woo, I promise you it's not. Even young children can grasp these ideas. And it can happen in short conversations.

You might begin with questions like, "What are you feeling right now? Where in your body do you feel this? What thoughts in your head go along with this feeling? What does it make you want to do? What would happen after if you did that?"

I think it's also wise, not to mention compassionate, to assure your kids that strong emotions like anger, grief, and discontent aren't wrong or bad unless we act them out in hurtful ways. Better yet, you can model what I've been talking about.

For me, this means that when I strongly dislike the way I feel, I take time to meet with myself for at least five minutes in my morning chair—or if I'm not home, some quiet corner. I take deep breaths, quiet my mind, invite Spirit to be present, and ask myself what I'm feeling and why.

How I wish my kids had even once stumbled upon me in such repose and inquired, "What are you doing, Mom?"

Imagine how my answer—"I'm letting myself feel sad right now," or "I'm asking God why I feel so irritable and bored" might have made a difference in their lives.

I hope I've said something here you find helpful, especially if you're one of those worried parents. I've been where you are. The fact that you care is huge. And it's never too late to for an entire family to wake up and feel their feelings.

Maybe waking us up is what our feelings are for.

In Memorium:
Hiding From Brennan Manning

During my secretive drinking years, I knew about Brennan Manning and even owned some of his books. Aware that he was an alcoholic as well as a Christian, I felt a certain affinity with him. At least on the page.

In person, it was a different story. Once I hid from him all weekend. It happened many moons ago when my husband Dave worked for a publisher that was reissuing one of Manning's older titles. Before the book's release, the publisher invited Manning to speak at a retreat for employees and their families.

I was in awe of his talent. I loved his message of radical grace, even if my inner addict couldn't afford to fully embrace it. But his presence was another thing. I was overcome by the irrational fear that he would take one look at me and recognize the secret drunk hiding behind the Christian costume.

Or maybe the problem went deeper. After all, Manning was someone I never, *ever* wanted to be—a person who publicly admitted to being alcoholic. Who could bear such shame? Plus, since he was a "recovering" alcoholic, this poor guy could no longer drink without major consequences. My worst nightmare.

As much as politely possible, I avoided Manning all weekend. While other people crowded around him after he spoke, I made myself scarce. When Dave ferried him back to the airport, I declined to ride along. I didn't want to catch what this guy had.

Now, I think it's kind of funny. And a little sad, too. Once I got sober, I pulled out all my Manning books and reread them. I couldn't believe that such tender words of hope and healing had been on my bookshelf all these years. (No doubt I'd hidden empties behind a few of his titles.) In one of them, I read:

> "In praying for chronic alcoholics, I'm frequently overcome by a surge of compassion that I don't ordinarily experience in healing prayer, perhaps because of my own struggle with alcoholism (which has been well documented elsewhere). The damnable imprisonment of not being able to quit, the obsession of the mind and compulsion of the body that paralyze the freedom to choose, the terror of human bondage, the nagging sense of hypocrisy, the guilt, the shame, the loneliness . . ."—from *The Wisdom of Tenderness*

I had been hiding from a man who already knew me well.

Recently, I picked up Brennan's memoir, *All Is Grace*. It's sitting right now on my morning table, where I start every day by lighting a candle and being quiet. I haven't cracked it open yet. And to be honest, I'm a little nervous to.

I think I'm a little afraid of that good kind of hurt; the kind an honest, broken "ragamuffin" writer can evoke; the kind that kisses a personal wound so tenderly that you ache and wonder if you'll ever be the same again.

But it's *good* to feel, I remind myself. It is good to not be numb. Numb is what keeps people like me hiding from people like Brennan. So here goes.

Dave Speaks
(a Q & A with my husband)

You sent great questions! Some of them we combined or edited for clarity. I didn't edit a word of his answers, though. He's pretty darn honest here, so my hat is off to him.

In *Sober Mercies*, Heather refers to "dumb drunk Heather fights," which sometimes led to physical attacks by her and often ended with her sleeping in the guest room. What was that like for you?

I hated the craziness and the violence. It tore me up inside—still does when I think about it. I didn't grow up in a family where people threw hateful words around, much less fists and boots. Heather grew up clawing to get what she needed, though. That was her way, and sometimes alcohol made her go there. In the craziest times, I would stare into the horror of what had become of us and see no way out. I didn't want to be married to her anymore. But I didn't want to start over again either (I'd already been a loser in marriage once). But when the smoke cleared, I would look across the room and see Heather Babe—not a monster. I really loved her. I've always been grateful that the affection didn't run out before the sobriety arrived! I know some aren't so blessed.

Did you know that Heather was an alcoholic?

I thought so, but I didn't know. Of course, I didn't realize how much she was putting away either. I would try to change her drinking habits by changing mine, including abstaining entirely for spells. That didn't work. She just got hostile and I got more resentful.

Why do you think you didn't catch on that she was drinking in secret?

She was a pretty good sneak. Most addicts are, I guess. Also, I didn't ever venture into her closet, which is where she kept her stash. Still don't go in there, by the way. She's not a neatnik—just sayin'. During those years, we drank together, and I often drank too much. That didn't help me know what was actually going on. And then there were the maintenance prescriptions that had been affecting Heather in one way or another since we met. When she got loony later in the evening, I blamed the meds.

How did you manage not to follow the same path as Heather?

I shared her life but, I don't share her genes. In a way, I'm living proof that alcoholism has a huge physiological dimension. Heather has as much willpower as me; she's as moral and as spiritual—not that we can really measure those things. Clearly, her body just reacts differently to alcohol.

Relapse is a common story in recovery. Have you ever worried that Heather would go back to her drinking? How would you handle that?

We've been there once, thanks to the Minneapolis airport. That and the aftermath were hell. I didn't know what would happen next. I was angry and afraid. I will be eternally grateful that she so quickly chose to start over again. I don't know what I'd do if she went out again. I don't like to think about it. Everyone who's married to an addict must worry about it sometimes. Honestly, I'm afraid to say anything that would appear to give her permission to do that again. But of course, I can't control her decision. It's hers to make. My job is to stay clean and sane in my own areas of blindness and weakness. There are so many. Day to day, though, I have a huge amount of trust in Heather. Her commitment to sobriety and spiritual health inspires me. I want to be like her when I grow up.

My husband is addicted to alcohol and drugs, and I don't know how to help him. He has failed so many times. What have you done to help Heather in her recovery? Is there one thing she would say has been most important to her?

I'm really sorry for about your situation. You must often feel helpless and afraid. I went through many years trying to figure out what to do to help Heather. Whatever I did try—talking to her, trying to delete alcohol from our lives entirely, suggesting counseling—didn't work. I didn't try an intervention, and maybe I should have, although I doubt she would have quit until she was good and ready. The day she told me sobbing that she needed to get help, I knew she was serious. After that, I did everything I could to get her into rehab before she changed her mind. Since she's been in recovery, she has said that my going to recovery meetings with her has been the single most helpful thing. On average, I probably go once every two weeks. She goes much more often, of course. But going together gives us a shared life and language, and many shared friends. And, hey, it feels like love to her.

How has being a part of Heather's program of recovery affected you personally or spiritually?

We're growing together—emotionally, spiritually, in our relationship—in ways that were probably impossible before. I mean, we were so much more stuck than we knew! 'Course, we're still freaks, but now at least we have a safe relationship. We have a home that isn't hiding anything. We have seen miracles in our family. We've gotten our life back. Every day is a gift, and I am filled with gratitude.

Finally, what advice would you give a spouse whose partner has an obvious problem with alcohol, drugs or addictive behavior of any kind?

Any of us can stand outside of that kind of situation and have the "right" opinions. But truly, there's no way for us to know what's really happening in that person's world. When the one we love is addicted, our choices—and especially our perceived choices—get all tangled up in love, shame, resentment, self-judgment, duty, habit and just what comes easier on any given day. Everybody's story is different, but here's what I wish I had done differently:

1. I wish I had taken the step myself to name and own the problem. I needed to fully face what was happening, and my part in it—whatever that was. I had things I was hiding too, things that needed more truth-telling. Like shame over how much alcohol had us in its grip, and my part in letting that happen. Like fear of what would become of us as a couple if we actually took the alcohol skeleton out of the closet.

2. I wish I had gotten help for myself. I needed to say, "I have a problem that requires outside help," and then act on the admission. I need to regularly drive off to counseling or Al-Anon—and she needed to see me doing it. It would have been a confrontation of sorts with our reality. She would have been outraged and disdainful, I'm guessing. And I doubt she would have changed any of her choices, but at least we wouldn't have been tacitly lying about the hell we were in. And more to the point—I would have been working on understanding my part in the craziness.

One thing I know now, looking back, is that there *is* a way out. Sounds so obvious, but I didn't believe that for years, and I know Heather didn't either. So many don't really believe change is possible—for others maybe, but not for them. But change *is* possible. And God will do for us what we cannot do for ourselves—we just have to let him. With humility and courage and a good dose of desperation, we *can* find the door. As Heather and I have discovered, that door opens to a recovery community that welcomes fellow desperadoes with open arms, shows us a proven path to living differently, and is willing to walk with us on it.

The Mothers on My Mind

I wanted to write a sweet piece for Mother's Day. I adore my own mother and would love to tell the world why. If you ask me, there's no greater proof of God's kindness and goodness on earth than a mother's love.

But I went to a woman's recovery meeting this morning. And so the mothers on my mind today are the ones who won't be celebrating or celebrated. The ones who know better than to hope for a big hug or coveted phone call, much less breakfast in bed.

I'm talking about moms who are estranged from one or more of their kids. Some, through their own bad choices—which doesn't lessen the pain, by the way. And others who, through no fault of their own, have had children ripped from their arms by the tsunami of addiction.

Last night Dave and I stumbled upon the movie, *Traffic*. We had seen it in theaters way back, but when I noticed the date—'99—I realized it would seem mostly new to me, since I was still drinking then.

I knew the movie was about drug trafficking. But I was still caught off guard by the brutal but oh-so-true depiction of the insanity and ironies of addiction: politicians fighting the war on drugs while swilling drinks; drug-lords gunning each other down over money; rich kids overdosing because even with money and privilege, life can seem meaningless.

It was impossible for me to watch this movie without thinking, *What on earth?! What is wrong with us? Why aren't we all more alarmed?*

And then, in a *Huffington Post* article, I read about a new report from the World Health Organization warning that alcohol kills more people every year than AIDS, tuberculosis or violence. If alcoholism or addiction looked like a bird-flu epidemic or jihadists, we'd call out the National Guard. We'd declare a state of emergency. We wouldn't think of carrying on business as usual.

But instead we sort of yawn and say, "Kids will be kids," or, "Damn junkies."

At one point in the movie, the new American drug czar—played to perfection by Michael Douglas—asks an official of the Mexican government, "What about treatment?"

"Treatment?" the guy says. "Addicts treat themselves. They overdose, and then there's one less of them."

Sounds cold-hearted, yet it reflects a commonly held view. As soon as a human being becomes a junkie, his value plummets.

Unless that junkie is your child.

Unless that alcoholic is your mother, spouse, or best friend.

So yes, these are the mothers most on my mind today. The moms estranged from their kids, maybe for forever. And the moms whose babies are out there somewhere, but nowhere really.

Are you one? On Mother's Day, while the world celebrates the awesomeness of moms—as we should—I just wanted to say that I'm thinking of you, and so are many others. You matter. You and your child are of infinite worth and beauty. And God has not forgotten you.

That's No Excuse

I met Joe—a cute 30-year-old salesman with red hair—at a seminar last weekend. As my student partner for a two-minute mock interview, he opened with something like, "So Heather, you used to be an alcoholic..."

And I said, "Yeah, but I'm still an alcoholic, always will be."

"Wait a minute." Joe looked baffled. "If you're still an alcoholic, why should I read your book?"

I quickly discovered that the disease concept doesn't translate well to a sound bite.

After the interview, Joe asked with a barely suppressed shudder: "But do you have to call yourself *that* word—*alcoholic?*"

It was a jarring reminder that outside my world of recovery, alcoholism still carries a stigma, and most regular folks don't think too highly of my kind.

Honestly, I don't blame them. I mean, addicts of all stripes have *earned* our reputation. Maybe no other people group has wrought more havoc, hurt more people, or broken out in handcuffs more often.

No wonder so many people "out there" resist the idea of labeling addiction a *disease.* Heck, people who suffer from cancer or multiple sclerosis don't go around driving drunk or selfishly laying waste to their closest relationships.

Plus, since we generally don't blame people for getting sick, calling it a disease could seem to imply that addicts aren't responsible for the harmful choices they make under the influence.

It's tricky territory, isn't it? I can't tell you how many times I've felt confused myself about a fellow alcoholic: *Is this woman a selfish, heartless bitch—or is she just super sick?*

I think the answer is probably both. Which is why I hope to make some distinctions that might help us find balance on this issue.

Addiction is diagnostically labeled a disease not because we innocently catch it like the flu, but because it is a physiological condition, it's often hereditary, and it tends to get progressively worse. Left untreated, it's often fatal.

Trouble is, most people don't realize they are genetically predisposed to a particular addiction until it's in full bloom. Like the smoker who contributes to his lung cancer, risky behaviors of addicts often play a part in the onset of addiction.

But that doesn't mean we get to blame the addict for being one. And it doesn't mean we shouldn't rush in to arrest its progress as soon as we can, since—as with most diseases—early diagnosis greatly increases the chance of recovery.

In a similar vein, while it's true that addictive compulsions compel people to do things they otherwise wouldn't, that doesn't mean that addicts are not human beings who make moral choices quite apart from their condition. Including the choice not to seek help.

This is why it's so important to understand addiction as a disease. In a very real way, it's good news for all of us. If addiction is a disease, addicts are more likely to understand that it's *treatable*. The alternative is to decide addicts are just fundamentally horrible people, and where's the hope in that?

Here's another thing. If we can fully embrace the idea that addiction is a disease, then we have a better shot at changing government policies to help sick people get well instead of just getting them locked up.

In the meantime, we addicts are the ones who must take responsibility for the choices we make. The verdict is in. While there is no permanent cure for alcoholism or addiction, *there is a solution.*

It's called treatment. It's called recovery. It's called meetings (which are free, by the way).

It's called redemption, Joe.

I'm Staying
for the Show

Dave and I managed to relax on our mini-vacation in Arizona last week, despite the fact that our hearts were breaking for those folks back home in the Springs affected by Colorado's worst wildfire in history.

In between checking the news on our phones, we went on hikes, floated in the pool, dripped dry in the sun, and let our brains turn to mush.

But that's not what I want to write about today. What interests me now about our trip are just a few small moments that spoke to me. Life is often like that. While we watch the horizon for big revelations, God drops a few wispy hints in our lap.

The first one came as we were driving down the road in our rental car. Dave swerved, I yelped, and we barely missed hitting a really big bird. Dave told me it was a roadrunner.

"But I always thought he was just a cartoon!" I exclaimed, which launched a discussion about how when you're a kid you somehow fail to notice that every single episode of that show is the exact same story: Wiley Coyote chases Road Runner, fails to catch him, and gets hurt or humiliated in the process.

Over and over and over again. I pointed out to Dave that this is every addict's story, too. We spend years chasing our drug of choice trying to capture a high that always just escapes us. No matter how many cliffs we fall from or boulders drop on our heads, in no time at all we're off again. *Meep, meep.*

Unlike Wiley Coyote, though, we don't magically recover from our injuries (and neither do those we injure). I know of a guy who relapsed this winter and ended up homeless in the snow, which led to frostbite, which led to gangrene, which resulted in his leg being amputated.

That's the difference between real life and cartoons.

A second moment happened on a hike with our friends. Susan (the same one I write about in my book, by the way) pointed out a plant to me. She said it was some kind of yucca in the throes of dying, and the big burst of flowers up top was its swan song.

"Just before it dies," she explained, "it sends all its nutrients to the top of its stalk for a big finale."

Naturally, I thought about that yucca while we hiked. Along the way, we spotted several more in similar dire straits. Or should I say glory?

I'm embarrassed to admit how much those desert flowers moved me. I thought of Jesus, the unexpected gift hidden in his dying. What little I know of surrender.

The last significant moment happened as Dave and I stood near a bush and watched a hummingbird whir. *How can such a tiny creature operate like a super-efficient helicopter?* Agasp with wonder, we agreed how foolish it would be to imagine for a second that we've got a grasp on God.

Who can explain all the mysteries?

But that was my vacation—a few small moments that hinted at something more. A roadrunner lives to see another day. A humming-bird makes it hard to look away. A yucca plant paints a picture of surrender.

I don't know about you, but I'm staying for the whole show.

When Mercy Trumps Judgment

Soon I'll be speaking at an annual fundraiser for a large women's center in Texas. Their mission is to provide housing and services to homeless and addicted women who are trying to rebuild their lives.

As I plan what to say, I realize I'll be speaking to a rare kind of audience: People glad to show up where they know they'll be asked to give money to help addicts and alcoholics.

Typically, you see, we're not a group that easily evokes sympathy. Our cause doesn't tug at the heart—or purse strings the same way child hunger or breast cancer does. And I get why.

To the casual observer, addiction looks more like selfishness at full throttle than a progressive disease. We addicts tend to be stubborn, manipulative, and in many cases, criminal. Some of us are known for squandering what help we do receive. No wonder we evoke disdain or distancing more quickly than generosity. Why would anyone want to throw good money after the likes of us?

Actually, I can think of several good reasons. More than two-thirds of American families are touched by addiction. It plays an enormous role in poverty, unemployment, crime, child abuse, and accidental death. The collateral damage is just huge. On the positive side, many of us do recover. An estimated 20 million people today are enjoying long-term recovery.

Yet, despite these numbers, we don't seem to have the collective will as a society to galvanize around this issue. It's as if the stigma attached to addiction extends even to our willingness to invest in recovery. And I don't see that changing until our compassion for the addict outweighs our aversion.

One of the biggest obstacles to such a shift is the erroneous belief that addiction is mainly a moral issue. Even though addiction is classified as a disease, many good people can't get past the idea that addicts choose their sickness. I get this. And it's true that addiction usually begins with bad choices and risky behaviors.

But trust me, no one sets out to become addicted. We set out to escape pain or feel better, unable—until it's too late—to conceive of a force so great it could hijack our brain and steamroll our will power.

And who among us hasn't felt desperate to change the way we feel? Who of us can be certain we wouldn't have become addicts ourselves had we been born in another place or time?

My plea for empathy raises another important point. Like a lot of folks, I used to assume that addicts were perfectly happy getting high or wasted or what have you. I had no idea they actually suffered.

When I spiraled into my own alcoholism, I learned the awful truth. Few people are more miserable than an addict who desperately wants to quit, but can't find a way to stop. Unless you've been there, it's hard to imagine what this kind of powerlessness feels like.

It feels like being stuck in a nightmare where you open your mouth to scream, but nothing comes out.

It feels like watching in disbelief as you begin to betray your conscience and your values, even as you pray to do the right thing.

It feels like knowing you're hurting the people you love the most—and knowing you'll do it again tomorrow.

It feels like losing your job, your driver's license, your home, your family and marriage—and still not being able to quit.

It feels like coming to believe you must have been born for nothing, since that is what you are accomplishing with your life.

Imagine feeling all of that, and I bet you'll agree that addiction isn't something any sane person wants.

And maybe it's time to let mercy trump judgment.

My Hat in My Hands

I wrote the piece about how mercy should trump judgment when it comes to addicts and alcoholics. Naturally, that same afternoon, I found myself sitting in judgment of a good friend, relishing unkind thoughts about how she's handling a situation that's none of my business.

Oh the irony! But the sad truth is, *I do this all the time.* I'm not sure a day goes by when I don't indict someone for what seems to me like a poor choice, a backward belief, or a self-created crisis.

Have I always been so arrogant, petty, and heartless? I'm afraid so. But hopefully what has changed is my willingness to admit it. Typically, when I catch myself in the act of judging someone, my first temptation is to scold myself: *Who do you think you are?! How dare you judge her! Shame on you!*

But you know what? That doesn't really help, because my ego is never going to feel sorry or try to reform. It just snickers at me and then stores away the negative energy for later use. And guess what? The only thing my ego enjoys more than bashing others is bashing me.

The good news in all of this is *we are not our egos*, and we are also not our thoughts. I'm convinced our true self is made in God's image, can't be diminished by anything we do or say, and only knows how to love.

So these days, when I notice my false self/ego is gleefully banging its gavel again, I'm learning to do two things.

First, I try to practice self-kindness; I look for a way to give myself a truer version of what my ego wants to take away from someone else.

Second, I look for the mercy angle—a shift in perspective that helps me arrive at compassion. I ask questions like: *What would it feel like to live in this woman's skin? What kind of emotional wounds might be driving her? How am I just like her?*

I like this version of "Be patient with each other, making allowance for each other's faults because of your love." (Ephesians 4:2 NLT)

I think *making allowances*—giving others and myself plenty of room and space in which to fall short or screw up—is a great definition of mercy. It's not at all the same as *making excuses*. You're not rationalizing away someone's responsibility; you're trying to understand what brought them to this place.

Of course, deciding not to judge someone is a lot harder when the person clearly deserves it; when we're not just annoyed or critical, this person actually *hurt* us.

In this case, mercy is more than a decision not to judge, it's a gateway to the more difficult task of forgiveness. But never is mercy more precious than now; and should we succeed, it can have a powerful ripple effect.

I experienced this first hand when I took my 9th Step in recovery. As I went about making amends to people I'd hurt, I noticed how the act of humbly going to people, my hat in my hands, asking for forgiveness suddenly made the idea of forgiving people who have hurt *me* seem remarkably *reasonable*.

I should hold my hat in my hands more often.

The Shame Slayer
and Anonymity

"Lasting addiction recovery solutions have been found, but the most credible faces and voices to support these solutions have been hidden and silenced for decades."
—From the movie, *The Anonymous People.*

The makers of this film are part of a passionate new movement which "aims to transform public opinion, engage communities and elected officials, and finally shift problematic policy toward lasting solutions."

I love what the film is up to. It brings to mind the term, "shame slayers," which I picked up from Glennon Melton.

But here's the rub. The film is causing a small stir in the recovery community around the long-held tradition of anonymity.

Since the creation of the 12 Steps in the 1930s, people in groups such as AA, NA, SLA, OA and others have worked to keep private their own and others' status as members. But recent years have seen a push by some to do away with aspects of this tradition that seem outdated and even counterproductive.

I don't think anyone in recovery is arguing the importance of protecting *each other's* anonymity. It's never my right to disclose another person's membership or association with any recovery group.

The movie itself is careful to respect this aspect of the tradition. And yet, the emphasis on the need for all of us to be more outspoken encourages a rethinking of anonymity with regard to press, radio and film. The tradition of anonymity at the public level is important, because it keeps any single person from becoming the "face" of our community. This in turn preserves our sense of diversity, protects our reputation from scandal, and prevents members from profiting via their association with the group.

But a lot has changed since the inception of the 12 Steps in the 1930s. Back then, the label alcoholic came loaded with a much fiercer stigma of shame and fear. Today, an increasing number of people are proud to be in recovery. Hiding in the shadows doesn't sit well with them.

Another huge change is that the advent of the internet and social media have blurred the lines between private and public media. What about my Facebook? Is that me talking to my friends, or me broadcasting to the world?

Finally, given the horrific epidemic of addiction in our society, it strikes many as irresponsible to be coy about the solution. It strikes some too as a contradiction of the organization's stated purpose: "To the carry the message to those who still suffer."

In some ways, the conflict surrounding anonymity reminds me of the story where Jesus is scolded by the Pharisees for healing a man on the Sabbath because "work" was forbidden on the Sabbath.

When rules or traditions get in the way of love, service, and compassion, hasn't something gone awry?

I don't think the recovery community is going to arrive at a consensus anytime soon. Individuals will continue to simply choose to do what they think is best.

And ironically, the very traditions we sometimes squabble over will continue to give us the freedom to do that.

When it Feels Good
to Feel Bad

On Saturday morning, my husband Dave and his son Neil took off in our pop-top camper for an overnight adventure. I was happy to see them go, thrilled to be left alone. I thought I'd get a lot of work done, or maybe have some fun hiking with friends. Instead, I sank into a swampy sadness that's been stalking me for a week.

Does that ever happen to you? Nothing's wrong. Really. But nothing's right, either. You think of numerous things you could do to lift your spirits. But some small, hard ball of rebellion in your chest resists the idea of trying to feel better.

So on Saturday, here's what I did. I watched *HGTV Design Star* on Comcast. All day long and into the evening, I hardly moved from my couch. When the most recent episodes ran out, I watched the entire previous season.

Oh, and I ate. And I ate. I stuffed my face with bananas dipped in chocolate, nachos drowned in cheese, frostbitten popsicles, and these gross Weight Watcher's caramels.

Once, in-between episodes, I got up off the couch and stepped outside and noticed how nice the air was. I could already hear myself saying to Dave—"Yeah, I spent some time on Saturday enjoying the beautiful day."

But then I turned around and went back inside.

Around 11 p.m., I learned who won Season 7 of *HGTV Design Star*. I don't recall her name now. But I do remember that just before I went to bed, I gorged on sweet potato chips.

I woke up Sunday morning thinking, *Okay, are you done now?* But I knew that I wasn't. Not by a mile. So I didn't go to church or to the recovery meeting we usually attend, either one of which could have threatened to ruin my bad mood. Same with God. I didn't think he'd approve of my having a pity party without a real problem. So he wasn't invited.

This is what a relapse looks like for me, minus the alcohol. It's a dangerous place to be if you're in recovery, since these kinds of behaviors—numbing, isolating, over-indulging, and cutting off God—are often precursors to a full-blown relapse.

But it's a human place to be, too. I don't know a single person who doesn't catch an emotional flu on occasion. Sometimes, there's little you can do but wait for it to pass.

In the meantime, you remind yourself that you know better than to believe your own thoughts. That what you want to do is probably not what you need to do. That your feelings, though important and real, are not the same as facts.

If your funk goes from bad to worse, or you sense you're on the verge of a relapse, it's time to go against your own will and reach out for help. Call a safe friend, or if you have one, your sponsor. And if you think you might be seriously depressed, go see your doctor.

As you might have gathered, I'm feeling so much better today. I woke up this morning ready to leave the swamp, ready to let go of enjoying feeling bad. I got on my knees and I told God, *I'm really sorry and please help me, I'm such an idiot and I don't know why.*

He suggested I take a bubble bath.

This Way is Better
(Or, Moms Who Drink Too Much)

One afternoon last week I was working upstairs in my hot, muggy office, trying not to suffocate, when I heard the sound of a can snap open. I yelled from my chair, "Hey, I heard that. Where's mine?"

My husband Dave was working from home that day. Moments later, he came into my office with an ice-cold can of sparkling water. I thanked him profusely and popped the tab. *Snap!*

"Remember when that was always the sound of a beer?" I asked.

"Heather?" he said.

"Yes?"

"This way is better."

Better, he meant, than when I drank daily.

Better than when I thought the best way to wind down, relax, or reward myself was with a glass of wine, a giant beer, or a gin and tonic. Okay, several actually.

Better than when I was hiding secret stashes of alcohol from him.

But I think Dave's remark meant more, too. Our life isn't better today only because I quit drinking. It's better because in our scramble to fill the empty spaces, we learned a new way to cope when life gets hard that includes gratitude, mindfulness, and tending to our spiritual growth.

Last week, one of you emailed me about several friends you're worried about. They tend to drink too much, you told me. And they say things like, "But drinking is a necessary coping mechanism to make it through my day as a mom."

Attached was a link to an article in the *Wall Street Journal* about the rise in drinking among women, mothers in particular. Apparently, it's become trendy to combine play-dates with happy hour, or to drink a few glasses in the afternoon before the kids get home from school.

Trust me, I totally get the logic. If it helps me relax, why should I feel bad about it? Maybe wine makes me a better mom!

But it also raises the question: is it okay for moms to cope with the stress and difficulty of raising kids by drinking?

I can't speak for other mothers, but I can share from my own experience.

My two boys were still school-aged when I began drinking in earnest. At first, alcohol worked so well! It soothed the exact nerves that my kids were always stomping on. It was easy to convince myself that I'd be more likely to harm my kids if I didn't drink.

But here's what I failed to reckon.

First, that I might be genetically predisposed to alcoholism and racing toward a nightmare.

Second, that a mom doesn't have to be visibly drunk or slur her words for her drinking to significantly affect her children.

What I know now is that kids sense it in their bones when you're not fully present. On some level, they know you're numbing your feelings and a part of you has gone missing—a part they have an inalienable right to—even if they can't put it into words until later. Even if they never can.

My kids were grown before they could name the ways drinking took me away from them. Ironically, though, the harm they felt didn't stem from my being an alcoholic or incidents of gross neglect. It was the way I used alcohol to create an emotional buffer between myself and other people, including them.

"You were always around," my grown son Noah once told me. "But you were never really there."

I was there for Nathan's football games, and Noah's concerts. I was there for prom, for homework, for dinners. Well, a woozy cartoon of a Mom was. But not me—not really.

If I could do it all over again, I wouldn't drink. I would work hard to find ways to cope or relax that didn't numb my feelings or dull my senses. And I would aim to stay fully awake and show up for the people I love.

Which is a pretty good description of how I'm trying to live today. Dave was right. *This way is better.*

On a Scale
of Numbness

In her book, *The Gifts of Imperfection*, Brene Brown explains how after working the 12 Steps for her drinking problem, she realized that alcohol was just one of the ways she compulsively sought to numb unwanted feelings.

She writes,

> "For me, it wasn't just the dance halls, cold beer, and Marlboro Lights of my youth that got out of hand—it was banana bread, chips and queso, email, work, staying busy, incessant worrying, planning, perfectionism, and anything else that could dull those agonizing anxiety-fueled feelings of vulnerability."

Today, Brown describes herself as a "take-the-edge-off-aholic." "But there's no meeting for that," she adds.

And she's right. One drawback of the disease model of addiction is that it fails to address the millions of people who seek to escape their feelings in ways that are troublesome and costly, but diagnostically don't rise to the level of addiction.

Brown suggests that all of us practice numbing behaviors, on a sort of spectrum, with addiction being at one extreme. It's a helpful idea, if you ask me.

Of course, not all flights of escape, indulgences or self-comforting tactics are harmful. But to the extent that they move us closer to serious addiction, nag at our consciences, depress us, or get in the way of our joy, they become problematic.

When I read this part of Brown's book, I immediately thought about my own numbing patterns. Just last night, Dave walked through the living room at about 8 o'clock and I cried out from the couch,

"Save me! Help! I'm watching the dumbest ever reality TV show and I can't stop."

I'd tell you what show it was, but I'm honestly too embarrassed.

So how do we know if a particular compulsion is costing us more than its worth?

Brown suggests we ask: "Does our [habit] get in the way of our authenticity? Does it keep us from staying out of judgment and from feeling connected? Are we using it to hide or escape from the reality of our lives?"

Maybe, I have to answer. *Sometimes.*

I say that not because a reality show keeps me from being real with you. But because on occasion, I do regret it. I go to bed annoyed at myself and far from enriched by the experience. Plus, I know the cost of a thing includes the loss of the better thing we might have done—or ate or drank or spent time or money on—instead.

I don't mean to imply that we should never luxuriate in dumb TV, waste time on purpose, or allow ourselves a second bowl of ice cream. It's really about trying to live intentionally, don't you think? And whether such choices become a chronic pattern.

As Brown points out, the real problem with take-the-edge-off behaviors is that it's not possible to numb selectively. When life loses its sharp edges, you are spared some pain, but you probably won't feel sharp pangs of joy, either.

Once we're intent on seeking comfort over growth, escaping our problems over processing them, avoidance becomes a way of life. We still have all the same pain and problems, only now they're muffled, leaving us feeling vaguely sad and—yet again—in need of escape.

Having tried life both ways—numb but safe versus raw but vulnerable—my choice is clear today.

I don't want to miss a thing.

Even in the Dark

On a recent morning walk, I asked Dave what he was thinking about. I expected him to mention one of our grown kids or else his work. But no, he was thinking about *trees*.

Dave likes trees a lot. He knows their names, where they grow best, and a whole bunch of other boring stuff about them. Here's what I know about trees: The ones with pointy sharp things might be pines. Oh, and they're typically green.

"I had a little revelation about trees," Dave continued. "But it might sound sort of dumb."

"Tell me," I urged. (I love it when Dave sounds dumb.)

He started with something I already knew—that he has been watching all week for new leaves on the trees. Spring has been confoundingly late this year, so it's been a long watch. (Last year, he suggested we throw a party to celebrate the emergence of leaves on the big trees that line our street. Seriously. You were almost invited to a Leaves on Our Street party).

"Anyway," he continued, "this time of year, when we get a warm stretch, they come out so impossibly fast. One day, no leaves; the next, leaves. How do they do that? And then it hit me. The leaves have been growing all night long. Even in the dark, the sap is still rising, doing its thing. I can't believe I just thought of that."

I laughed and agreed that it seems rather obvious. But of course, I couldn't resist the also rather obvious spiritual metaphor. "So do you think *we* grow at night too—in our soul, spiritually—even while we're sleeping?"

"No," Dave answered quickly.

"Then again…" He thought a moment. "I guess that's a pretty ego-centered response, isn't it? To assume that I can't possibly grow unless I'm *thinking*. Like our minds do all the work, not God."

I don't know about you, but I often forget this. Years after mov-ing out of a faith culture that promised more holiness as a reward for more effort, I still sometimes forget that I am powerless to trans-form myself. I want to believe I can see a defect of character, and then take steps to fix it. I'm grateful for God's help, sure. But my version of transformation has *me* in control. Me taking credit, too.

Think my way to change? It might sound promising until I remember that my best thinking got me drunk. What I learned in recovery—and I'm embarrassed to admit it came as a surprise—is that changing me at my core is God's job, not mine. In recovery, we open ourselves to the miracle of transformation in many ways, but perhaps none more directly than when we say the 7th Step prayer. It goes like this:

> "My Creator, I am now willing that you should have all of me, good and bad. I pray that you now remove from me every sin-gle defect of character that stands in the way of my usefulness to you and my fellows. Grant me strength, as I go out from here, to do your bidding. Amen."

Of course, we all have a significant part to play in our spiritual progress. We get to do our best to create the ideal conditions for growth to take place in our soul. We get to read spiritual books, pray and meditate, and take part in a spiritual community that will tell us the truth.

But maybe the most important thing we can do is act like trees. Let our roots go down deep into the ground of God's love. Let God's Spirit flow like sap into our being. Believe he's at work, even in the dark.

It Was Me Who
Reached Out for You

I heard from a couple readers who know they're addicts or alcoholics, but just can't find the willingness to reach for help. Their emails came with heartbreaking confessions. One began, "I'm drinking as I write this…"

I've so been there: you know you have a problem, you're desperate to quit, you might even see the end coming, but *you're not quite ready to give up and reach for help.* It's such a miserable place.

In recovery we say, "It takes what it takes." But we also say, "You reach the bottom when you quit digging."

Another common thread in the emails I've been getting is fear of embarrassment or rejection. I so get that, too. It was a huge part of the reason I spent so many years begging God for a huge private miracle. I wanted him to zap me from heaven and declare in a booming voice, *Your faith has made you well, Heather! Go your way and drink no more.*

Or better yet, *"Go your way and drink no more . . . than two glasses a night."*

The point is, I wanted my miracle my way.

I see a little of myself in the woman in the gospel story who'd been bleeding for twelve years. She thinks—correctly, it turns out—that if she can just reach out and touch Jesus' garment, she'll be healed. And no one will know.

But Jesus did know. He turns around and asks, "Who touched me?"

His disciples give him a funny look. "Uh, gee. We're, uh, walking through a crowd?"

But Jesus persists. "I felt power flow from me," he says.

Trembling with fear, the woman steps forward to confess that she's the one who reached for him.

I'm pretty sure Jesus already knew this. And I wonder if he didn't also know that naming her need in public was somehow a necessary part of her healing.

I was sober for a couple years before I understood that God's power to heal and help me had been there all along. I simply couldn't receive the miracle because I wanted it on my own terms—in a way that would spare my pride.

And what if God *had* chosen to deliver me *my* way? It would have been wonderful. I could have returned to my old life, relieved and grateful. *Whew! That 'being a drunk' thing was awful! I'm so glad I'm past that now!*

But God would have gotten little credit. And I would never have gotten into recovery, or written about it, or fell in love with the wonderful sober friends I had over for dinner last Tuesday night. I would never have come to understand how good it is to have to rely on God utterly, and on a daily basis.

Today, I'm so grateful that God in his kindness waited for me to say yes to healing on his terms and in his way.

And the miracle *is still going on.* I experience it every time I grasp again for the dusting of grace that lies heavy on God's cloak.

Every morning, I hear Jesus ask, "Who touched me?"

And every morning, I get to answer, "Me, Lord. It was me who reached out for you."

Faces Unashamed

The reason I love authors like Brené Brown and Glennon Doyle Melton is their willingness to be vulnerable on the page—even as they teach us how to be vulnerable in our lives.

Vulnerability isn't as easy as we can make it seem. At least, it's not for me. I'm entirely capable of using apparent transparency—*Look at me telling you everything!*—as a shield, a trendy trick, an invitation to make you say, Look how real she is. Sometimes, I reek of authenticity.

The reason all this matters to me so much is that as a recovering alcoholic who once lived a double life as a secret Christian drunk, my message has a lot to do with coming out of hiding and getting honest with myself and God and others.

At the heart of my story is a battle with shame and the power of a lie that told me that I would literally *die* of mortification if anyone ever knew my secret.

What I've since learned is that shame is what happens when we hide, not when we finally show our faces.

A favorite of mine in early sobriety was this verse from Psalms: "Those who look to him are radiant; their faces are never covered with shame."

The greatest shock of my life was to discover that the exposure of the very secret that I thought would kill me brought me the greatest relief. It turns out that when you give up on looking good, no one can make you feel bad.

This is part of why I wrote *Sober Mercies*. Because when I am determined to hide, I harm myself, and in a roundabout way I hurt you too. When I smile and pretend that I'm okay even though I had a huge drunken row with my husband last night, some part of you hears me say, "It's not okay to not be okay."

We hear a lot of talk these days about people coming out of the closet. I rejoice every time some brave person decides to risk everything on the crazy hope that people will love them as much if not more when they learn who they really are.

I was in the closet—*literally*—for more than twelve years. My perpetually messy closet was where I hid my alcohol inside my tall boots or wrapped inside old sweaters. I often drank there, too—standing in the dark, guzzling as fast as I could so that my husband wouldn't miss me downstairs.

It takes what it takes for most of us to come out of hiding. But here's what else I'm learning: Big secrets don't matter any more than smaller ones. It's not so much the surrendering up of salacious affairs or headline-grabbing hypocrisy that makes us honest.

What matters is one woman saying to another, "This is how I really am today. How about you?"

Let's walk in the light together, with faces unashamed.

Surrender the Bone

I lived as a secret slave to alcohol for more than twelve years. By day I wrote Christian books on topics like marriage and prayer, and by night I got blotto drunk. I can't think of anything I treasure more than the freedom *not* to drink today.

But freedom is a mysterious thing. Honestly, in the context of addiction, some of what the Bible says about it barely makes sense to me. Take for example, "So if the Son makes you free, you will be free indeed" (John 8:36).

I always took this verse to mean that once you become a Christian, while you might still feel tempted to sin, you could never again be a *slave* to sin. But if that's true, why do so many Christians end up battling addictions?

For years, I couldn't figure it out. These days, I wonder if the answer isn't as simple as this: Now that God has set me completely free, I have the power to say no to slavery. *But I also still have the power to say yes.*

Which is what I did with alcohol, one sip at a time. Of course, I thought I could stop drinking whenever I wanted—right up to the point when I couldn't, no matter how hard I tried.

I've told this story before but it's my favorite picture of this awful dynamic. In African streets, the monkeys were often a terrible nuisance. The native boys developed a proven technique for capturing the critters. They'd tie a chicken bone inside of a hollowed out gourd, making sure the opening was too small for a monkey's hand *and* the chicken bone to come out together.

Next, they'd fasten the gourd to the base of a tree. Soon enough, a hungry monkey would follow its nose to the gourd and reach inside to grab the bone. Now the boys would draw near with their nets. Sensing danger, the monkey would screech in terror. But instead of fleeing, it would cling to its prize . . . *unwilling to let go of the bone.*

You don't have to be an addict or alcoholic to identify with the monkey's dilemma. Clinging is what we humans do most naturally. Give us something that looks, tastes, or feels good, and we'll go to almost any length to keep it—often, even when it endangers our freedom.

Jesus famously told his followers, "If you cling to your life you will lose it..."

So why do we still hang on? I wonder if it's because letting go feels a lot like *dying*. It hurts so much. It seems way too hard. But as Jesus reminds us, it's our desperate clinging to an empty substitute for life that will ultimately rob us of the real thing.

But here's good news. Unlike those monkeys in Africa, we don't have to find the courage or will to surrender our bone on our own. We can fall to our knees and cry out to God for rescue. And we can demonstrate our *willingness* to let go by accepting any help he sends.

Six years ago, when I finally sought treatment for my alcoholism, I felt terrified and embarrassed. I hated to admit that I couldn't stop drinking by myself. But in rehab, I met a bunch of beautifully broken people who were just as baffled by their addiction as I was.

As I listened to their stories, I heard them telling mine. Slowly, my desperate grip on alcohol began to loosen. Then one day, I saw a fellow monkey who was stuck and scared. I reached out my hand to help her, and I must have dropped my bone.

I never picked it up. Today, I'm still free.

I Dream of Drinking

just had the worst drinking dream of my life.

I came down for coffee just reeling from it. Dave was there and rubbed my back and helped me feel a little better. But manoman.

It wasn't one of those dreams I've had in recovery where I accidentally drink or even one where I know I've relapsed—the panic of what I'll do now. It was the old kind, the kind where I am desperate and frantic and people are everywhere who would stop me and I keep thinking I see people I know in this house/hotel/store/restaurant (it kept changing). I kept trying to figure out how I was going to buy alcohol and get it to my room without people seeing. In this dream, I guess there was no such thing as grocery bags? :)

The scariest, weirdest part of the dream was how much I was physically craving alcohol, that intense, sobbing feeling in my pit of my stomach, in my veins, in my hands, even. Like my whole body was dying of thirst literally.

I couldn't decide which would taste better, wine or beer.

I could imagine the sharp tang of each and it tore me apart to have to choose. I decided to get plenty of both and I kept thinking I should call someone, maybe someone could help me. But then I couldn't drink and I HAD to drink.

And then I woke up. In THAT state.

Of course, reality floods in and is such a relief cognitively. But the rest of you—your emotions, your heart—is still in the dream. Like when you dream of your husband hurting you horribly and you wake up with all this achey, painful emotion. Like that.

I keep wondering where it came from. I got an email from a woman yesterday—or at least I answered it yesterday—who is going to meetings and trying so hard to quit and stay sober and keeps wanting to

Sober Boots

"sneak." She was saying how much that part of my story spoke to her, the urge to get away with something, and so I was remembering that feeling when I wrote back. That could have tipped something inside.

But here's the thing. I woke up from the horror of my dream SO apologetic in my mind to every alcoholic who has ever reached out to me and I've made it sound too easy. *Just reach for help, go to treatment, or go to a meeting.*

I was so keenly aware of how intense the pain is—and craving *is* pain, I'm telling you—and how fortunate I am that I don't live in this state of constant terrible *want* anymore. But not living in it anymore makes it so easy to take this for granted!!

Oh dear God, I am sorry I have so thoroughly forgotten how tight that grip is and how real the cage is and how dark is that darkness when your only relief seems like it has to come from the one thing your entire body is begging for—including every nerve and emotion.

No wonder alcohol is so appealing, since it is the only drink that can escape your stomach to soothe and be felt in your psyche and soul and every cell in your body.

I feel shaky and sick right now.

I couldn't go to my meeting last night unless I walked, which seemed too hard, so I didn't go. I left my car keys in the hotel room in Georgia and so my car is sitting at the shuttle hotel until the housekeepers send the keys; so the only car I have is Dave's old Mercedes and it was on empty with the light on and it takes diesel and after obliviously driving it yesterday without looking at the gauge—I was too afraid to even try to get to a gas station.

But I could have called someone. I could have got on my bike, for goodness sakes. I should have gone. Not that this would have prevented the dream, though . . . who knows.

What to make of the sneaky thing?

I wrote to this women how I thought that for me it came from this intense desire to get something I wanted but felt barred from, a rebellion of sorts, a grabbing for something I desperately needed but wasn't being ALLOWED.

218

Also it had to do with the intense conviction that if I didn't sneak, I was going to be deprived of something good—no not good, *necessary*.

Deprivation is a mindset that takes us under, that lie that something vital is being withheld.

I wish I could I recall when in recovery I stopped feeling this and how, but honestly all I can say is that at some point I finally decided it would be so much easier to *not* want this thing and I finally quit drinking in my head and heart. I finally faced the fact that it was poison to me, so it was pointless to pretend it wasn't and torture myself.

Somewhere along the way, God lifted that obsession—to the point where I no longer cared about alcohol even if it was right in front of me. It just doesn't exist.

Dear God I hope that will hold after this dream I had. That was my terror really—when I was half awake—this horrific fear that what if it came back? What if God allowed me to suffer temptation that intensely again in real life? What would I do?

Maybe I shouldn't be writing here when I haven't processed all of this clearly yet, but my first thought after I got coffee was, m*aybe someone needs to read this.* Maybe someone else out there forgets, too. Maybe it will help someone feel less alone in the agony of wanting what they can no longer have safely.

If that's you reading this, I am praying for you. Right now.
For all of us.

Dear God, it is so hard to live in this world where that thing in us that is against us makes us desire to have our way, to take what we feel we need, to indulge and comfort ourselves in a way that leaves you out.

Please help us. Please help many who are desperate for a way out today. Please forgive me for forgetting how much this hurts. Please bring this pain to mind with sufficient force as often as I need to experience it so that I care deeply enough to have utter and complete compassion on every man or woman who reaches out for help.

I don't want to forget, I don't want to take a single sober day for granted, as if I paid my dues and now I'm out of jail and it doesn't matter that so many are still there, as if they have it coming or any of us do, or any of us deserve to spend even a single day in that prison.

We are confounded, God. Confounded by the irony of being in love with what we hate. Please rescue us. Please help us to surrender. We can't make it on our own. Oh how we have tried! Oh how real that part of us is that wants to give up for good. I know we are each precious to you. Bring us home, God.

At the Intersection
of Addiction and Grace

On Monday I flew to Virginia to speak to a gathering of Salvation Army officers who operate their addiction rehabilitation centers in the Southeast. I was pretty nervous about it. I was also deeply grateful for the opportunity.

My grown son Noah joined me on the trip, and I can't tell you how much it meant to have him with me. As we sat at a gate waiting for a delayed flight and Noah was tracking his fantasy football teams on his phone while eating a huge bag of airport popcorn, I was overcome by joy.

Just to have him next to me. Alive. Sober. Just to have him squeeze my shoulder now and then and say, "You're going to do great, Mom."

How can this be the same young man who used to smoke pot for breakfast? Who I used to fear would turn out like my father—addicted, depressed, and suicidal?

How can I be the same mother who used to drown my worry about Noah's drugging and drinking by getting drunk myself? Who used to live in dread of being exposed as an alcoholic and would rather die than declare it from a podium?

The only explanation is that Noah and I are walking, talking miracles—living proof of God's goodness and grace.

This was never so clear to me as it was on Monday as I spoke about the role of faith in my journey of recovery. Noah graciously allowed me to share some parts of his story, too—including how he'd probably be dead if the apartment where he was living when he hit bottom had had a garage.

After I spoke, we had a buffet lunch with the Salvation Army folks, and I noticed how easily Noah chatted with people. Several times I overheard someone ask him hopefully, "So do you speak, too?" He laughed and said no.

But you know what? He does speak. His life speaks. And nothing speaks louder than the story he can't help telling just by being who he is today.

At one point, a man whipped out his wallet to show us a photo of a ragged-looking young man. "This here is 'Frank' before," he explained, meaning before he came to their program. "And this is him after," he said, showing us a photo of a clean-cut, smiling man who now works for them. He couldn't have been prouder had he been this guy's father.

When I was invited to speak to the Salvation Army, initially I was perplexed. What came to mind first were the thrift stores I spent half my childhood trapped in with my bargain-loving mother. What came to mind next were the red donation cans and the tinkling bells at Christmas.

And then, I thought of my father. Mentally ill and addicted, he spent the second half of his too-short life homeless, in mental hospitals, in halfway houses—*and in more than a few Salvation Army rescue missions.*

Early in my recovery, I attended a meeting downtown where the "Sallys"—the men participating in the nearby Salvation Army rehab program—reminded me of my father. Their stories touched me deeply for this reason, but also because the changes in their lives were often so dramatic. I'd listen in near disbelief, thinking, *You mean to tell me this articulate, hard-working man was living under a bridge just a year ago?*

Sadly, my dad wasn't one of these success stories. He never found recovery for long, and he took his own life at age 47. No one ever pulled his mug from their wallet to show how the program works.

Yet in Virginia, I was struck by the sweetness of God to bring me to speak here, and especially with Noah along. It felt like coming full circle, like *this* was the real end to my dad's story.

Best of all, I got a chance to look some of these folks from the Salvation Army in the eye and say a belated, *Thank you.* My father was hungry and you fed him. My father needed clothes and you clothed him. My father was homeless and you sheltered him.

This is what it means to stand at the intersection of addiction and grace.

For the Loved Ones

A while back I wrote a piece for addicts who can't seem to surrender called, "The Hunger Games, Hope, and Hitting Bottom" (page 62). This morning, I feel compelled to share the other half of that message.

It's for the loved ones of addicts and alcoholics who may have heard an incomplete message about your role. The message goes something like this: I am completely powerless to help the addict I love, and the only thing I can do is stay out of the way until he or she "hits bottom."

It's absolutely true that in trying to help we can unwittingly enable an addict or shield him from the very consequences that might spark a change. Wisdom is required, for sure. Alanon exists in large part for this reason—we can't change another person; we can only change ourselves. But none of this means we should do nothing while a loved one spirals ever further toward tragedy or death.

This topic is very personal to me. As most of you know, my oldest son began a scary descent into alcoholism and drug abuse in his teens that continued into his twenties. When he was 21, a worried friend of his alerted us that he was drinking himself to death—literally. We scrabbled together a small family intervention and got my son into a three-month treatment program. He loved sobriety and was excited about the future. Then, on his first night out of rehab, he drank. He couldn't explain why, and he didn't get sober for another five years.

But here's the thing. Despite the seeming failure of that intervention, who can say what seeds of hope were planted during his stay in treatment? Or whether, when he finally hit a horrible bottom years later, his memory of that time wasn't part of the reason he reached for help? If your loved one is in serious trouble with addiction, you may want to consider an intervention, too.

An intervention happens when family and friends of an addict create a plan to lovingly but firmly confront an addict and urge him or her to get into treatment. Some families enlist professional help, while others go it alone. Of course, many interventions fail. The addict refuses to accept help. Or, the help doesn't seem to stick. So why bother going to all that trouble and expense? Here are seven reasons why an intervention might be worth the risk.

1. Addiction is a progressive disease that only gets worse if left untreated and is often fatal. Especially with kids and young adults whose brains are still developing, a delayed response diminishes the chance for a full recovery. Waiting for a teen to "hit bottom" can be like waiting for stage 2 cancer to get to stage 4 before starting treatment.

2. Interventions are often necessary to save lives because a hallmark of addiction is denial and resistance. Why would we let a clear symptom of a dangerous disease keep us from trying to get help for the sufferer?

3. Some addicts and alcoholics have to get sober for a while in order to realize they actually want to be sober. That's why rehab or even jail can turn a person's life around. The fog of insanity lifts enough that they can willingly reach for recovery.

4. Turning points don't have to arrive on the heels of great devastation or loss. Paradoxically, they can also be chosen. In recovery we say, "The bottom is where you decide to get off the elevator," and, "The bottom happens when you stop digging."

5. Despair, shame, and mortification alone won't bring most addicts to the point of change. Often, these painful emotions merely fuel the cycle of self-hatred and self-sabotage, reinforcing an addict's fear that they don't deserve to recover. A loving intervention can be a powerful message in this context.

6   For most of us, a low point does not become a turning point unless hope is part of the picture. With no view to a better life and nothing to lose, an addict can bump along a series of should-be bottoms for years. A strategic intervention by loved ones can point the way to a life that's worth staying sober for.

7   Without intervention, many addicts simply won't hit bottom until they're six feet under—or have put someone else there. I often look around the room at all the years of sobriety represented in a recovery meeting and try to imagine what carnage the world has been spared.

Regardless of outcome, stepping in to urge treatment and set boundaries is a way of showing an addict just how far they've fallen at the same time that you're showing them how deeply you love them. Being part of such an event can be a profound, even sacred experience. If it doesn't change the addict, it might change you. I realize that I've only touched the surface of a complicated issue, but I hope this list will spark some thinking. If you know someone who loves an addict, pass this message along.

Her Pretty Little Neck

One recent afternoon, I was sitting at my desk feeling lonely and anxious when I noticed the sun was shining through the blinds in a way that felt perfect on my face. I shut my eyes and basked in the light. For the next few minutes, I let everything go and invited God to mend the achy places in my heart.

Instead, he broke it open further. Which has been happening a lot, I've noticed, ever since I started asking God to help me grow in compassion. I should have known his answer would be to allow me to feel other people's pain in a very real way.

The person on my heart that afternoon was a friend who relapses often and has recently been taken out again by her alcoholism. She's someone I tried hard to help once and had to let go of before I acted on the urge to wring her pretty little neck.

In the past couple of weeks, God's been prompting me to call her again. And I've delayed, telling myself I wasn't sure I heard clearly. But sitting there with the sun on my face, I realized the real reason behind my reluctance: I enjoy my cushy life too much.

The thought sort of shocked me, but I knew it was true. I've gotten so comfortable in my safe little bubble of recovery that I've totally lost touch with the gritty, hard work of loving sick people who can't love you back. Sure, I sponsor women. But they're all my friends, too. They're perfectly nice, do the work, and make me feel good about myself.

Meanwhile, I notice I no longer go out of my way to help the hard cases, invite new people to lunch, or give my number to the jittery girl who just got out of detox. It's a scary realization, since there's no quicker way to lose your sobriety than to stop giving it away.

So, I called my friend with the pretty little neck and left a message. It's been a couple days and she hasn't called back. No great surprise. It takes a lot of hope to pick up the phone, and I'm pretty sure she's low on that.

She's been in this cycle for years, you see. Rehab after rehab, relapse after relapse, and in between, promising periods of sobriety that often end in a seedy motel or in the ICU.

When she's not drinking, she tries to find meetings where no one knows her—which is getting harder and harder. I can't imagine how humiliated she must feel at times. To be that person, the one everyone knows can't seem to stay sober. The one everyone knows has left in her wake a trail of people who tried to help and only got worn out.

Today, I'm wondering where she finds the courage to keep coming back. To try one more time. She might be the bravest person I know.

I also keep thinking about something Jesus said, "What credit is it to you if you only love people who love you?" And it dawns on me, even as I write this, that maybe God's not asking me to help my friend because I can make a difference, but precisely because I probably can't.

Maybe this is where compassion begins.

My Sister's Addiction

A few mornings back, I came upon an excerpt from a book my sister sent me a couple years ago, along with a note that said: "This is me! This is me!" Here's what she sent:

> "I have been learning that the life of a caretaker is as addictive as the life of an alcoholic. Here the intoxication is the emotional relief that temporarily comes when answering a loved one's need...
>
> While much good can come from this, especially for those the caretaker attends, our care itself becomes a drink by which we briefly numb a worthlessness that won't go away unless constantly doused by another shot of self-sacrifice...
>
> At the heart of this is the ever-present worry that unless we are doing something for another, there is no possibility of being loved. So the needs of others stand behind a bar that, try as he or she will, the caretaker cannot resist..."
>
> —From *The Book of Awakening* by Mark Nepo.

I think sending this was my sister's way of saying, See Heather, I have compulsions, too! We're not so unalike. I understand you and your alcoholism, but do you really understand me? I need to be needed because that's what feels like love to me. Something clicked. I understood for the first time ever that I'm not the only one whose compulsions have cost me. My sister has paid a high price for her addiction to self-sacrifice: As long as she kept impulsively giving, she couldn't grasp that she'd still be loved even if she gave nothing.

During my active alcoholism, not surprisingly, I took my sister's care-taking nature for granted. Since she liked to be selfless without expecting much in return, I thought I was doing her a favor by cooperating. When on occasion she complained that she was more invested in our relationship than I was, I blew her off as being too needy and over-sensitive. So what if we don't talk unless she calls me? So what if I forgot the plans we made? Why did she have to take things so personally?

Thankfully, I've changed a lot, and my sister has, too. But both of us had to hit "bottoms" around our compulsions and seek outside help to discover a healthier relationship.

Still, escaping old patterns has been difficult. It's just so tempting to go into default mode and play a childhood role. Katherine is the dutiful, good girl who takes care of everybody. Heather is the snotty brat who manages to get away with murder. These roles have been so engrained in us since childhood that trying to change them has at times felt like trying to knock a marble out of a deep groove by simply blowing on it.

Still, more and more, we are learning to love each other with conscious intention. She keeps healthy boundaries and doesn't take my occasional thoughtlessness so personally. I affirm her importance to me and do my part to tend our relationship. It's not perfect, but it's a beautiful process.

We all know addiction and codependency tend to run in families. But guess what? Recovery does too!

The Promise of Shared Brokenness

I get a lot of emails from people who've read *Sober Mercies*, which means so much to me. But I keep noticing how one particular line from the book keeps coming up. Last week, after three people in a row quoted the same sentence, I went back to read it in context:

> "The particular brand of love and loyalty that seemed to flow so easily here [in recovery meetings] wasn't like anything I'd ever experienced, inside or outside of church. But how could this be? How could a bunch of addicts and alcoholics manage to succeed at creating the kind of intimate fellowship so many churches have tried to achieve and failed?
>
> Many months would pass before I understood that people bond more deeply over shared brokenness than they do over shared beliefs."

Aha! Clearly, a lot of you have shared my experience—felt a lack of community in a church setting or been surprised by the depth of community in another kind of group. I think my conclusion resonated because it hints at the reason why. After lots of thought, here's a more developed theory:

- When folks gather around a system of shared beliefs, the price of acceptance in the group is usually agreement, which means the greatest value—stated or not—is being right. Unfortunately, this often creates an atmosphere of fear and performance, which in turn invites conformity.
- But when people gather around a shared need for healing, the price of acceptance in the group is usually vulnerability,

which means the greatest value—stated or not—is being real. This tends to foster an atmosphere of safety and participation, which in turn invites community.

I'm not saying recovery or support groups are good and church groups are bad. But I do think the latter could learn something from the former about how to create safe places where intimate community can happen.

Of course, we all face the same challenge on how to foster authentic connection. As much as our souls crave it, our ego fears it.

For most of us, it's fairly easy to share intellectual head space with someone: We know this, we think that. Not much risk there. But inviting that person into our heart space where we may feel broken in places takes courage, sometimes even desperation.

Last week, a recently widowed friend of mine came to stay in our guest room for a week. As much as she was tempted to isolate at home, she had the bravery to finally admit she needs to be around people right now, and let them into her grief.

And here's the beautiful part. Dave and I needed this, too. Since all our kids are long gone, her presence in our home felt like a gift. Having her join us for dinner or watching TV—she in her pajamas— gave us a dose of that family feeling we keenly miss.

I find myself thinking about the cross in the context of connection. How the Old Testament Law failed to bring mankind close enough to God. How God sent his Son to die so he could make his home in our very soul.

Maybe God understood that we bond more deeply over shared brokenness than we do over shared beliefs—not just with each other, but with him, too.

A Lot
More Beautiful

I t seems my piece about bonding over brokenness versus beliefs hit home for many. It also raised the question: So what could the church do better to create connection and community?

I don't pretend to have all the answers. Let's agree that many churches do work hard to provide the kind of openness and safety that invite intimate fellowship. And of course, beliefs and brokenness aren't mutually exclusive; you can embrace both, and most Christians I know try to do this.

The point I hoped to raise is that sometimes it seems like we care more about what people believe than we do about loving them. And when "right beliefs" become the basis for inclusion in our fellowships, some of the most broken among us don't feel welcome.

Maybe this is part of why the church Dave and I go to now has no official creed. In fact, when our pastor baptizes babies, in addition to the traditional things you'd expect to hear, he says, "We will not presume to tell you what you have to believe..."

The first time we heard this, we glanced at each other in alarm. What on earth? Isn't that the purpose of church—to make sure we believe all the right things—and all the same things—about all the important things?

Up to now, we hadn't realized Christ-centered churches like this one existed. Churches that welcome everyone. That care about tradition but don't double-check your doctrine at the door. That have enough faith to believe that God is present and at work in everyone's journey.

It was a lot to take in. Yet we also found comfort in knowing that if we decided to stay, we wouldn't have to agree with anyone's theological, social, or political leanings in order to worship together, or to be accepted and loved.

We knew we had finally found home there the first time we celebrated Communion. When the pastor held up the loaf of bread and invited us all, something in the way he spoke about Jesus being broken and given brought tears to our eyes.

Recently, Dave and I got to facilitate a month of adult Sunday school classes around the topic of addiction, recovery, and faith. The first Sunday, I shared my journey from out-of-control drinking into recovery. Another Sunday, Dave shared his side of the story.

We looked at the (dismaying) statistics about the prevalence of addiction. We looked at Scripture (Paul had a thing or two to say about doing—over and over again—the very thing he hated.) But given the topic, it was such a relief to know no one was evaluating our spiritual correctness or critiquing our theology. We got to be vulnerable about our mistakes and weaknesses, and people responded in kind.

It got me wondering what might happen if we did this kind of thing in church more often. Maybe sharing our actual stories—what life was like, what happened, what life's like now, and what doesn't look like it's freaking ever going to get better even though we're following Jesus—would help to foster the kind of rich community so many find in recovery.

The power of truth telling to free us and change us can't be overestimated. And hearing one another's stories is how we realize we're not alone, and that it's okay to be human.

Mysteriously, when we share our shattered and less shiny parts with each other, our differences disappear. Healing happens. Community blossoms. We become a little more whole—and a lot more beautiful.

Worried About
All the Wrong Things

This week I'm spending a lot of time working on a speech I'll give soon—practicing the delivery of it on my computer's video cam.

Wince is too sweet of a word to describe what it's like to watch it. If, like me, you still want to believe folks who say you don't look your age, I can't recommend this approach. Trust me, it has occurred to me that I might just be worried about the wrong things. It's not about me, right?

In typical, self-centered fashion, I had imagined that treatment would be all about me. I had pictured myself spending a lot of one-on-one time with the staff psychiatrist while he probed my psyche to solve the mystery of what drove someone as nice as me to drink myself blotto. Sure, I knew the other patients would be there, hovering in the background. But in my mind, the camera was always focused on me, front and center.

It was nothing like that. I quickly learned that rehab is nothing if not a group activity. It's like one long experiment in the study of how people develop intimacy with strangers. Naturally, whether or not this is a good thing depends largely on who your fellow residents happen to be. These are the people who will see you with bed-head at six a.m. when you stumble half asleep down the hall to have your vitals taken. Who will learn your most shameful secrets. Who will see you exposed for what you are—a blubbering drunk in Banana Republic clothes.

Who won't like you.

It was true. Right away, several of the residents decided I thought I was better than them. During dinner in the school-style cafeteria that first night, a lesbian and meth addict named Geneva mocked me for being so "put together." She said I looked like one of the damn counselors. She was sure if I met her on the street, I wouldn't give her the f*@*#ing time of day. Others at the table nodded or snickered.

I had half-expected this—not quite fitting in. But I was taken aback by the open hostility. I went to my room and cried.

What did these people want from me? Should I *not* put on makeup and blowdry my hair? Should I wear only T-shirts? Forgive me for not knowing what a "tweaker" is! (It's a methamphetamine addict.) *I don't think I'm better than any of them!* I insisted to myself.

And yet, I did think I was *different*. I just wasn't in the same category as these hard-core alcoholics and drug addicts. I'd never stolen anything. I'd never spent time in jail or on the street. I'd never woken up naked in Vegas, unsure how I got there and who was in bed with me.

That night, I phoned Dave and told him I'd met a drug-addicted lesbian named Geneva who hated me on sight. I told him I missed him. I missed Edmund (my dog). I missed being at home in our house on our wide, pretty street where no one ever looked at me funny, wore pajamas to dinner, or asked me what I was 'in for.'

On the upside, before I came to treatment, I had envisioned myself curled up in a corner, sweating profusely, delirious with pain, and perhaps suffering small seizures. But that never happened. Much to my relief, during those first couple of days, I was given some medication to help me cope with the physical symptoms of withdrawal.

In the meantime, because I was new and detoxing, I was temporarily excused from most of the program activities. Since I didn't have a roommate, this allowed me plenty of time to wallow in self-pity. In fact, I was so worried about being ostracized that I forgot to worry about not being able to drink.

At around eight on that first night, the irony hit me. Instead of climbing the walls with craving as I'd expected, I was alone in my room, calmly reading a book, desperately upset because a lesbian didn't like me.

Obviously, I had worried about all the wrong things.

P.S. Just so you know, Geneva turned into a great friend and I eventually realized I was *exactly* like all the other residents.

The Key
in Our Hand

Some days, writing about addiction and recovery gives me so much joy. Other times, it feels impossible. How can I write helpfully about such a baffling subject? I'm reminded of a line in a Rumi poem:

"One of the marvels of the world is the sight of a soul sitting in prison with the key in its hand."

Isn't that so true? It's one of the most crazy-making aspects of addiction—how it seems to us (and others, too), like freedom is clearly within our grasp. Just use the key, quit the addiction, and walk out of jail.

If only it were that simple. Instead, we scream bloody murder to be rescued, and then run at the first sign of help.

It's hard to explain, except to say that addiction seems proof of our split nature. In the grip of compulsions, we become a soul divided— part of us wants to surrender and part of us fights to hold on. The demoralizing tug-of-war that results is surely one of the main reasons addicts tend to hate themselves so thoroughly. Add to this an endless series of self-inflicted wounds, humiliations, and losses—and you can imagine how shame fuels the engine of addiction.

Unfortunately, prevailing wisdom says the addict must exper-ience *ever more painful* consequences, tragedies, and heartbreak—until they finally hit rock bottom and become willing to change.

I agree that *desperation is necessary for surrender.* But sometimes I wonder if we've arrived at an incomplete conclusion. If "hitting bot-tom" alone is the magic bullet, how come so many addicts suffer one devastating blow after another—and still don't recover? What hap-pens when all you have left to lose is your life?

After years of hearing addicts' stories, I have a theory of my own.

Sober Boots

I think most of the time a low point doesn't become a turning point unless an addict hits bottom and hope at the same time.

Hope looks different for each of us, of course. For me, hope looked like meeting Susan, who happened to be in recovery. Her obvious zest for life gave me reason to believe that sobriety didn't *have* to be equal parts deprivation and misery.

For a bunch of women in Amarillo, Texas, hope looks like a place called the Downtown Women's Center, where I'll be speaking. They provide *long-term* help to homeless and addicted women so they can rebuild lives *worth staying sober for*.

Part of what I'll be trying to say is how hitting bottom *without hope* mostly leads to despair and too often, death. But hitting bottom *with hope* can lead to surrender.

And that's when we notice the prison key in our hand.

No Matter What
(For Moms of Addicts)

This time, she's wearing a floral dress and pink lipstick. The pained expression I recognize well. Before she even opens her mouth, I'm pretty sure she is the mother of an addicted son or daughter.

I meet this mom too often, I'm afraid. This particular one I met on Tuesday, after I spoke. She's scared out of her mind, guilt-ridden, and confused. How could this happen to her baby? And her worst fear is too great to voice: *I'm terrified my child is going to die.*

I'm scared her child will die, too. In the U.S. alone, addiction and alcoholism kill on average 300 people a day, many of them young. That's a jumbo jet filled with passengers going down. Every. Single. Day.

The hardest part might be that I can't even tell this mom, "Trust God—it's gonna be okay." Because it might not be. Ask any parent who earnestly prayed for God to protect their child and then said goodbye in a morgue.

Despite what some of us—including myself—have been taught, God really can't be trusted—not for specific outcomes. No matter what a parent does, or how hard we pray, anything can happen, including our worst nightmare.

Life is fatal, you know?

Which is just not tenable, especially for us moms. Which is why I don't often talk about the divine trust problem with other worried mothers of addicts.

But maybe I should. Six years ago, facing this issue head on helped me turn an important corner with my own alcoholic son. A turn toward more peace of mind and, I might add, a more honest relationship with God. It happened like this:

For years, I was terrified that I would lose Noah to an alcohol or drug related accident, overdose, or suicide. He was out of control, spiraling down. Days and nights, I pleaded with God to save him. Which was a right and good thing to do. I believe in prayer, even if I don't understand it.

Then, one rainy afternoon, I finally had a breakthrough. I saw that God could not be trusted to keep Noah safe or alive—and yet he was asking me to release my son to him, anyway.

As you can imagine, that didn't feel safe. At all. But neither did the burden of continuing to believe that if I just prayed hard or long enough, or said the right words, or lived the right way, I might twist God's arm to save my son.

Mine was a tearful, agonizing surrender that afternoon. It meant giving up on the comforting notion of a God who proves his love to us by intervening on our behalf in the ways of our choosing. It meant banking everything—*even my son's life*—on the truth that God is always and nothing less than love *no matter what happens on earth.*

It was the hugest relief, and today I understand why. Surrendering people we can't control anyway liberates us—and *them.*

I didn't automatically stop worrying, of course. And my decision to let go didn't mean that even *after* Noah was in recovery I wouldn't again despair, feel afraid for him, or desperately try to bargain with the universe. We're never going to stop being moms, right?

If today you're one of those moms with a heart full of pain about a child lost to addiction, I'm so sorry this is happening to you. And I believe God is too. Surely, his compassion for mothers of addicts is greater than we can even grasp.

But I encourage you try. And to cling fast to hope even as you let go. Maybe the best gift you can give yourself is to put your hope in God's unfailing goodness . . . *no matter what.*

Secretly Hoping
for Edmund's Demise

When I was newly sober, I had a list of possible tragedies which, should they come to pass, I thought would warrant a relapse. Surely, if my husband died or I got terminal cancer, no one would begrudge me a drink, right? But since part of me *hoped* for such an excuse, I amended the list to include the more bearable scenario of my dog Edmund's sudden and tragic passing. :) Which might explain why twice during my early recovery Edmund was almost killed due to negligence on my part. Once a car hit him because I had him off leash. Fortunately, he's so small he bounced off the front spoiler and rolled away to safety.

Another time, while lowering my passenger seat for a nap, I inadvertently pushed Edmund out the rear window and onto the freeway. Fortunately, traffic was stalled and we noticed he was no longer in the car before we drove off.

If you're an alcoholic, you understand why I used to think, *When's this little rascal gonna die so I can drink?* Today, the idea that I might drink seems unlikely—a fact which, ironically, makes me more vulnerable to relapse. Especially when you consider I never saw it coming when, at six months sober, I drank at Dave in the Minneapolis airport.

So, in the spirit of vigilance, here's an unscientific list of conditions that may increase our risk of relapse.

We have a history of slipping. The more we relapse, the more relapse starts to feel like an option we can come back from—until we can't.

We were active in our addiction for many years. It makes sense that the longer we used or drank, the more deeply ingrained those patterns of behavior can be, and the harder to break.

We have been in recovery a long time. It's true. The longer we stay sober, the harder it is to remember our powerlessness, and the easier it is to think we've changed enough that we could handle a drink.

We have a lot of YETs. We haven't yet got a DUI. We haven›t yet lost our job, our kids, or our marriage due to our stupid habit. Yets are good news until they make us wonder if we're *really* alcoholics or addicts like the rest of those people we meet in meetings.

We aren't part of a recovery community. Most of us just can't do this thing alone. We need the support and accountability that comes from being vulnerable with—and deeply connected to—others on the same journey.

We take prescription meds that can be addictive. For many alcoholics and addicts, this is a slippery slope that takes us right back to our drug of choice.

We keep our recovery secret from friends and family. If the most important people in our lives wouldn't know or care if we relapsed, we probably don't have enough at stake in our sobriety.

We live or work in an environment rife with "triggers." Repeated exposure to situations that weaken our resolve—for example, excessive stress, anxiety and conflict—set us up to seek relief in our bad old ways.

We think we're beyond danger. There's a big difference between healthy confidence and the kind of cockiness that results in complacency. The latter is likely to lead us to a drink.

We are unwilling to seek outside help. Many of us get sober only to discover we need to address other mental health issues, which if neglected, can threaten our sobriety.

We fail to take the actions our program suggests. We rely on God to keep us sober, but God relies on us to do our part.

Unless we take the steps historically proven to help, our sobriety is likely to be precarious.

We don't help other alcoholics. We often remind each other in meetings that we keep what we have by giving it away. Assisting newcomers reminds us of the nightmare we've been saved from, and helping others gets our attention off of ourselves.

You know what? Reading through this list right now, I realize that at least three of these apply to me today. This doesn't mean I'm doing anything wrong, it just means that like everyone else in recovery, I need to stay vigilant if I want to stay free. By the way, don't worry about Edmund. Let's face it, he has good reason to believe he'll live forever. In the meantime, I no longer secretly hope for his demise. And if he dies, I promise not to drink at his funeral

Another Coconut Cake

Yesterday the last of my family who were here for my 50th birthday flew home. I hoped I'd wake up this morning with something amazing to say to you about aging with grace, the wisdom of years, or the spiritual meaning of wrinkles. Instead, I feel worn out, uninspired and, um, thicker.

I blame the coconut cake. The large, moist, yummy-beyond-belief one from a bakery in town. Since I got only one slice at the party, I had the brilliant idea the next day to buy another one to celebrate my daughter-in-love's upcoming birthday. After that celebration, we kept the rest of the cake on the island in the kitchen. For the next couple days, I unofficially ate coconut cake for breakfast, lunch, even for between-meal snacks.

One afternoon, my daughter-in-law caught me standing at the cake, my fork loaded in mid-air, not a plate in sight. I was embarrassed—until she laughed and said, "I've been doing that all day, too. That's my fork on the counter." Now you can see why I love this girl so much. And you can also see why I might never again as long as I live want another bite of coconut cake. Which gets me thinking today about the difference between over-indulgence and addiction.

I can't tell you how many times I drank wine until I it made me sick. Or worse, felt compelled to drink even though I was already sick. *But not once did I lose my taste for alcohol.* It's as good a proof as any of the insanity of addiction—and that I'm not addicted to coconut cake.

Still, it was a good reminder that I'll always be vulnerable to compulsive behaviors that bring pleasure in the moment but leave me with regret.

This morning, as I totter about with a fresh pound of frosting around my waist, I wonder why I did that. Why did I find it necessary to treat my body so recklessly? What painful feeling was I trying to numb? Maybe I was nervous about having all these people here to celebrate…me? Maybe I figured I had earned the right, thank you very much, to pig out on my birthday. Or maybe, quite possibly, *I just adore coconut cake.*

One of the hazards of spending so much time thinking and writing about recovery issues is that I can get too serious, sifting everything through the grid of addiction.

Sometimes, the truth is simpler. Maybe I'm spiritually flat today because, for almost a week, it's been hard to pray and meditate in my office when a daughter or sister is sleeping there on a blow-up bed. Maybe I'm emotionally weary today because I'm companied out.

Last night, I made it to my first meeting in a week. I had little to contribute, apart from this truth: "I'm really sick of Heather. It feels like it's been all about Heather for weeks. And yet, at the same time, I miss my own soul. Does that make sense?" They all nodded.

That's how I know it's going to be all right. As long as I don't see another coconut cake again. Forever. Okay, for a couple weeks.

A Lesson From My Roomba

One of the best gifts I got for my birthday is a Roomba. If you're not familiar, it's an amazing little machine that vacuums carpets and floors *for* you. When it's done cleaning a room, it automatically returns to its home base to recharge its batteries. Or at least, that's how it's supposed to work.

The first time I used Roomba, I made a common mistake. I left the base outside the room where it was vacuuming, and so it couldn't get home to reboot. Finally, it simply ran out of juice. Which reminds me of my life some days.

The way I zoom around, rushing to do what I vaguely hope is God's work—but without relying on God's power. By the time I notice I'm worn out and spinning in circles, it's hard to find my way back to center.

Jesus told us, "Come to me, all of you who are weary and carry heavy burdens, and I will give you rest." I've always loved this verse, but recently I noticed something new. The promise of rest is contingent on the invitation, "Come to me..." Lately, I've felt too busy to come. I've been distracted and anxious, intent on getting ahead of the day before it starts. Clearly, some part of me doesn't really believe that resting in God is more productive than racing around.

A few weeks ago, I was whining to myself about how busy I was when a strange thought popped into my head: *Busy is an attitude.* It sounded like something an annoying blogger (like me) would say. Or like something God might whisper in *someone else's* ear.

It took me a while to see the logic of the idea: Sure, stress is real. And some of us have more pressing tasks than others. But since we're all allotted the same number of minutes in a day, and none of us can live more than one moment at a time, in one sense, *we're all equally busy*. It's when I try to carry around in my head an entire week's worth of to-dos that I get overwhelmed and have a *busy attitude.*

Perhaps this is why in recovery we so often remind each other to simply "do the next right thing." If I try to live ahead of where I am, I teeter under the load. I also become scattered and discombobulated.

Yesterday, I was late for an appointment with my sponsor. A short time later, I spaced out on a lunch date with a dear friend. Normally, my best excuse would be that I'm *busy, busy, busy!* I'm doing important things for God, you see. I'm such an important person I can't help it if I forget little things like *appointments with people I love.* ARGH.

Clearly, it's time to take a lesson from my Roomba and return to home base. It's time to get back to that secret place of stillness and prayer where God restores my soul. It's time to hear again God's gentle invitation . . . *and come.*

He had tried many ways to quit smoking
but only one worked.

Ditch
the Gas Cans

When I first ran across this cartoon, it totally cracked me up. It's hilarious the lengths some of us are willing to go in our battle against destructive compulsions. But if you think about it long enough, it's sad, too. The desperation depicted by our guy with the gas cans is all too real for millions of people who can't find a way to beat their addictions.

I can't tell you how many times I've heard stories of addicts who, in a reckless bid to disrupt their disease, consciously or unconsciously put themselves and others at risk of death. Still other addicts take drastic measures that can only be called ill-advised.

A few weeks back, I got a frantic email from a mom whose heroine-addicted son had just left her house to go commit a crime in hopes it would land him in jail and "give him a break from his demons." She didn't know what to hope for. I didn't know what to tell her. But I understood that son's twisted thinking.

When I finally entered treatment, I too—or at least some small part of me—welcomed the idea of losing access to alcohol. For me, though, it was about revenge. After so many years of failing to conquer my Inner Drunk, I couldn't wait to watch her finally *lose*.

As it turned out, what helped me most had little to do with not drinking. What mattered more, what made all the difference, were the bonds I formed with fellow sufferers. A line from our recovery literature says, "Almost without exception, alcoholics are tortured by loneliness." *Tortured* is the right word, by the way. Especially since our favorite solution to loneliness is to further isolate ourselves in drink. Which makes me wonder: What if Gas Guy's biggest problem isn't that he can't quit smoking, but the fact that he's trying to quit on his own?

It's no coincidence that every successful recovery program I've ever heard of places a premium on community. Treatment modalities differ, but they all understand and harness the same mysterious power of one addict talking honestly to another.

Today, you might feel a lot like our guy with the gas cans. You've tried everything you can think of to control or outwit your addiction, or punish yourself for having it. So far nothing's worked. You're beginning to think it's time to play high stakes poker. *What if I stacked the deck so high that if I drank, everything I cared about would go up in flames? Would I pick up then?*

You probably would. Here's a radical idea to try instead. What if you went to one of those meetings *specifically designed to help people just like you with your exact problem?* I swear to God, we don't bite. Very few of us smell bad. Sure, sometimes we cry. But mostly, we share our stories and laugh a lot.

Quit Deeper

It's been about two weeks now since I told God, *I want to quit.* I wasn't even sure what I meant by that, but God's response was quick. He said, "Quit deeper."

Quit deeper? What's that supposed to mean? The best I've been able to come up with is that while I want to quit a bunch of stuff out there in the world, God wants me to quit a bunch of stuff on the inside. Like trying to control other people, caring what people think, or demanding to know what's next in my life.

This morning, during my prayer and meditation, I was ready to do that. I've worked myself into a place of self-reliance again that I hate.

It always happens the same way. At first, I don't even notice I'm taking control. Then an enormous wave of anxiety and tension builds—sometimes for days and weeks—until I can't wait for it to break into the sweet relief of surrender.

I felt sure that wave was cresting, so I whispered to God: *I quit. I quit. I quit.* But it didn't work. Something inside of me still held tight, like a cold fist clutching my sternum.

Which brought to mind an old 80s movie starring Michael Cain called, *The Hand.* (Yeah, this is how my meditations go). It's about a guy, an artist, who loses his hand in a car accident. Weirdly, no one can find the severed hand at the scene. That's because—*yep, you guessed it*—the hand is still alive! Soon it starts to crawl around all by itself, committing terrible acts of violence. (The movie is more funny than scary).

But seriously, sometimes this is how I feel about my spiritual life. It's like I keep hacking off this egocentric, diabolical part of myself, and it keeps coming back to torment me. (Okay, I know I'm mixing metaphors again. Is it a *wave* that needs to break or a *hand* that torments? Sorry.).

This morning, after I couldn't find a way to let go, I got angry. At myself. At the way I keep ending up here.

Then it finally hit me. Maybe *quit deeper* means more than my usual, periodic surrender. *Maybe I need to surrender to the idea that I'll always need to surrender.* Ack! I hated this thought.

You see, secretly I cling to the hope that if I just keep trying harder, someday life won't feel like life. Part of me is convinced that there's some spiritual trick or breakthrough or technique that, once mastered, will allow me to live in a perpetual state of surrender, inner peace, and freedom.

Maybe we all dream this dream. We imagine being so enlightened that ordinary days will no longer make us restless. Busy days won't throw us off balance. We'll even welcome criticism and failure, because we no longer care what people think.

But that's not going to happen, is it? So maybe *quit deeper* means we get to stop believing God made us to be to be anything other than human. Maybe *quit deeper* means we get to stop listening to the voice that tells us God would love us more if only we tried harder.

Maybe *quit deeper* really means, *Come closer.*

The Aftermath
of Surrender

I don't know about you guys, but I excel at spiritual insights I can't manage to implement. No matter how hard I try, the gap between what I know in my head and how I live that out keeps getting bigger. I know it's a human thing, not a Heather thing. But sometimes it bums me out.

Last week, though, a chance encounter with an old friend shifted my perspective a bit. I hadn't seen him for ages and was anxious to catch up. For the past year or so, he told me, he'd felt certain God was preparing him for a specific role in a particular ministry. A few weeks ago, they hired someone else.

"It felt like the bottom dropped out of my life," he explained. "I ended up sobbing on the floor in front of my wife." His honesty surprised me. In the past, I think pride would have kept him from disclosing such a personal disappointment. He would have put on a brave face for everyone but his wife. Instead, I've never seen him more relaxed, real, and open.

At one point he said, "I don't understand God. I don't get life. I don't get how any of it works, anymore." But he said this without a trace of bitterness, and even with some relief.

The longer we spoke, the clearer it was to me that my friend had undergone a huge surrender. He's been forced to let go of a dream, to relinquish spiritual certainties, and to accept that God's will is infinitely mysterious—and often disappointing, to us.

And yet, I'm tempted to say he seemed happy. Not the kind of happy that comes from getting what you want, but the kind that comes from giving up on what you want altogether.

As tough as that sounds, I almost felt jealous. It made me want to undergo a similar humongous surrender. But not really, of course. Because surrender itself is bloody, hard work.

What I really want is to live in the *aftermath* of surrender. That peaceful place where you're finally okay with whatever happens to you or doesn't. You have nothing left to lose because you've let it all go. No one can hurt your pride because there's none left to protect.

Let's be honest, though. Most of us experience only a handful of these kinds of huge surrenders in our lifetime. One of my biggest came in 2007 when I finally became willing to get help for my alcoholism.

Since then, it's been a series of smaller but necessary surrenders. I say, *necessary*, because as much as I try to abandon myself entirely to God every morning—I tend to renegotiate as the day unfolds.

As you know from a previous piece, God's been encouraging me lately to "quit deeper."

At first, I thought this would look like something really big. A major surrender to rock my world. Instead, it's turning out to be a series of small relinquishments and capitulations: *How can I let go here? What do I need to accept? What would giving up look like?*

But maybe that's okay. Maybe "quit deeper" happens one small shovel of surrender at a time. And maybe the gap between my best intentions and my ability to carry them out is part of God's plan, too. And it's his grace that fills the gap.

"Does Daddy Drink Because I'm Bad?"

Because Daddy's sick."
Throughout my childhood, this was my mother's explanation to my siblings and me for why our father behaved erratically, why we had to move across the country to get away from him, and why he was no longer part of my life.

On the one hand, I applaud my mother's wisdom. She was on the right track with "sick." It described my father's chronic drug addiction and mental illness in a way that didn't denigrate him or make us kids feel like we were to blame for his absence.

But at the same time, without further elaboration and discussion, *sick* left me a bit confused. In my child-mind, *sick* was what happened when you got the flu. It didn't change how you behaved, and it didn't make people want to divorce you.

Never once in my memory did my mother use the word "drug" or "addiction." An unintended, unfair (to her) consequence is that I grew up furious at her for leaving my poor, *sick* daddy. "You should have waited for him to get better!" I'd shout.

Of course, today I understand my mom did the best she could with what she knew—and she probably deserves an award. Especially when you consider how back in the 70s, she had few resources at her disposal and there wasn't near as much awareness around addiction.

It wasn't until seven years ago, when I got into recovery for my own alcoholism, that I began to grasp the complexities of the disease my mother had been up against. Now I get how hard it must have been for her to understand my father's chronic relapses and empty promises—much less explain them to four little kids.

Even in our more enlightened age, discussing addiction with a child can sound like an intimidating proposition. Especially since kids are bound to ask painful questions like: *Does Daddy drink because I'm bad?* or, *Why doesn't my mom love me enough to stop taking pills?*

But the importance of educating ourselves and getting comfortable with such conversations can't be overstated. Kids need to process out-loud just like adults do. And the child of an alcoholic or addict probably needs repeated reassurance that their parent's unloving behavior has nothing to do with their own worth or lovability.

I recently got acquainted with a mother in recovery who stayed sober long enough to finally regain custody of her blonde toddler son. For months, she faithfully brought him to meetings, sitting him on her lap, kissing the back of his head dozens of times in the course of an hour.

A few weeks ago, she showed up without her son in tow. She'd had a bad relapse, and her boy had been returned to foster care.

Needless to say, this child has a long road ahead of him. And I can only hope and pray that somewhere along the way a compassionate adult will talk with him in an age-appropriate way about his mother's alcoholism.

Note: Resources you could check out: Carolyn Hannan Bell's books, *Daddy's Disease* and *Mommy's Disease: Helping Children Understand Alcoholism.* By doing what their subtitle says, both of these books fill an important gap in resources for families affected by substance abuse. Honestly, I think these books are just as helpful for adults who don't know what to say as they are for kids who don't know what to think. The mom and dad in these two stories gently lead the way and show you what to say.

I know I've only brushed the surface of a big topic here.

What Can I *Not* Say?

Something I read today from Parker Palmer really resonated with me. The book is called, *Let Your Life Speak.* Which is kind of the opposite of how I tend to communicate truths that resonate with me. My approach is more, *Let Your Mouth Spout.*

I did that the other day when a depressed friend came by for a visit. She was in that place where you wake up and realize you have nothing to give and you want the world to go away.

I gave her some great advice and shared spiritual tidbits that seemed inspiring to me. I was gratified when she told me, "I wish I had a tape recorder."

It wasn't until hours later that I realized I missed the real opportunity—to listen with kindness and care. To give her space and time to arrive at her own wisdom. To help her soften around her pain instead of suggesting it's wrong to feel this way.

In *Let Your Life Speak*, Palmer writes about his own struggle with depression.

> "Twice in my forties I spent endless months in the snake pit of the soul," he explains. "Hour by hour, day by day, I wrestled with the desire to die . . . I could feel nothing except the burden of my own life and the exhaustion, the apparent futility, of trying to sustain it. I understand why some depressed people kill themselves: they need the rest."

Naturally, lots of people tried to help Palmer. To cheer him up. To remind him how valuable his life was. To suggest ways to break out of his funk. And not surprisingly, none of it helped much. He writes:

> One of the hardest things we must do sometimes is to be present to another person's pain without trying to "fix" it, to

simply stand respectfully at the edge of that person's mystery and misery. Standing there, we feel useless and powerless, which is exactly how a depressed person feels—and our unconscious need is to reassure ourselves that we are not like the sad soul before us. In an effort to avoid those feelings, I give advice, which sets me, not you, free. If you take my advice, you may get well—and if you don't get well, I did the best I could. If you fail to take my advice, there is nothing more I can do. Either way, I get relief by distancing myself from you, guilt free.

I can't tell you how often I've done that, how easily I forget that sometimes the only thing more powerful than just the right words is just the right silence. The kind that *bears with,* not *bears* advice. The kind that inspires small, powerful acts of love.

"Blessedly," Palmer writes, "there were several people, family and friends, who had the courage to stand with me in a simple and healing way. One of them was a friend named Bill who, having asked my permission to do so, stopped by my home every afternoon, sat me down in a chair, knelt in front of me, removed my shoes and socks, and for half an hour simply massaged my feet. He found the one place in my body where I could still experience feeling—and feel somewhat reconnected with the human race. Bill rarely spoke a word."

This seems like a good challenge for me next time I'm with a friend who aches: How can I honor the sacredness of her struggle? What can I do to *show* that I care? What can I *not* say? Let's hope it's a lot.

Days and Slips and Chips

This email I received brings up a difficult issue I've been tempted to write about it, and finally will:

Hi Heather, I hope you are well. I want to ask you about a situation, if that is ok. I recently had a "slip". I drank late one night after 120+days, resumed my sobriety the next day. My feeling is that, though not continuous, the transformation I have made in my life has been miraculous. I abused myself for years with booze, and though I feel disappointed that I drank, I feel like it is time to stop with the self-castigation. I screwed up . . . I am trying to learn to be kind to myself. I don't want credit for what I have not achieved. At the same time, I don't want to be discredited for the changes I have made. I have not found a lot of resources or support for this scenario in the recovery world. It has pretty much all been "you are back at day 1." Is it only about the "days"? Do you have any thoughts on the subject you would be willing to share?

Congratulations on your sobriety and your honesty. As your note points out, counting continuous, unbroken days of sobriety and picking up milestone chips is an honored tradition in recovery groups. I think the purpose is threefold: to encourage people to stay sober, to celebrate hard work, and maybe more important, to show newcomers that long-term sobriety *really is possible.*

That said, this ritual rubs some people the wrong way, and I understand why. Whenever you introduce what looks like a system of reward, by default it can seem to punish, as well. For example, in some groups the chairperson asks at the opening of the meeting if there is anyone here with less than 30 days of continuous sobriety. The idea is to get to know newcomers and hand out "desire" chips. But it can also be used as a device to let the group know if someone has had a relapse. When a person with long-time sobriety raises their hand at this juncture, it can feel like they're being publicly outed.

When I relapsed after 6 months, my sponsor (I didn't even get a chip til after the relapse) told me I should raise my hand at every meeting when this question got asked until I had more than 30 days. Regardless of the good intention, it felt humiliating, and almost like punishment. But because humility and rigorous honesty had been so stressed to me, it felt wrong to do any less.

In the best of circumstances, this kind of public accountability can be helpful, I suppose. Some people say that the fear of having to tell everyone about a relapse keeps them from relapse. But I question whether that's sufficient—or even a good—motivation to stay sober. Fear of humiliation only takes us so far.

A couple months after my 6-month relapse, I got in a huge fight with my husband while family was here and wine was out on the counter. On impulse, I grabbed an open bottle, planning to chug—but after one gulp, stopped. Halted by the horrible specter of yet another relapse, I corked the bottle with a sigh of relief. At the time, I was naïve enough—or blatantly in denial enough—to call it a close call, not a relapse. I didn't tell my brand new sponsor and I forgot about the incident until many years later—actually, I came across the memory while writing my book.

When I let my sponsor at the time read it, she felt hurt and deceived. She accused me of harboring a dark secret and insisted I change my sobriety anniversary date by the two months and tell my home group what happened. I didn't have any problem with her suggestion—and did so promptly. But I did object to her thinking the worst of me.

Ironically, in retrospect, I'm so glad it wasn't clear to me then that a gulp of wine is a relapse in the eyes of my program! Had I thought of it as such, especially given my recent relapse in September, I am absolutely positive I would have drank that entire bottle, been furious at myself, and would have decided that since I was back at Day 1 anyway, I might as well get good and drunk. And who knows how long that relapse might have lasted. Instead, my naiveté (or intentional denial—who knows?) sort of saved me.

So what am I saying or suggesting? I'm not sure, but here are some things to consider. The whole thing about chips and counting days can be helpful—or it can be harmful, depending on the person and their experience with reward systems, guilt, and the like. For me, coming from a conservative Christian background, it hinted at the kind of legalism I was trying to escape. It reminded me of how quickly churches or Christians erect all kinds of unwritten rules that have nothing to do with Scripture and everything to do with culture. Or human nature.

I think it's our egos that prompt us to set up systems that help to measure who's doing it right or wrong, who's losing and who's winning, who is the "strong Christian," or who is working a "strong program." So we turn suggestions into commandments and value a practice we've come up with more than the principle that inspired it.

There's nothing in the core literature of the most popular 12 Step program that suggests handing out chips and such. Or for that matter, that even talks about sponsors, much less sets them up to be the boss of another person's sobriety. The role of a sponsor is to help take you through the 12 Steps and acquaint you with the program. Sponsors share their experience, strength, and hope. But given our human natures—both to want to be told what to do and to want to tell others what to do—you're somehow a better recovery soldier if you have a hard-ass sponsor.

I'm sure you've noticed tons of other unwritten "rules" in recovery having to do with a myriad things. Some of these are helpful. And sponsorship, if you ask me, is extremely helpful, too. But we do ourselves and the program a disservice when we become strident about any of these things and let them take precedence over love and grace and yes, live and let live. We encourage folks to take what works and leave the rest—but we forget to warn them we might freak out if they do.

More and more, I find myself shying away from those who want to turn their recovery into a religion. Those who want to believe there's only one right way to do anything. Given our diversity, we need more grace than that. So what's my answer about slips and chips and "days?" I know of many folks who simply stopped caring about or taking chips because they don't want to participate in that aspect. I have a sponsee who hasn't taken a chip in years because she feels an aversion to it—and since she's doing marvelously, why would I try to force that on her?

That said, I *do* take chips. I enjoy celebrating my friends' and my milestones. But those who love me know that I personally celebrate April 4 as my Miracle Sobriety Birthday—not Nov 24, my official sobriety date that commemorates that dumb gulp in the kitchen. The April date is the day my life changed, the day I walked into a treatment center, shaking in my bones, terrified but made brave by desperation. That's the day that changed the course of my life and it's also the time of year I experience all my anniversary feelings.

But out of respect for a program God used to help save my life, I take my birthday chip on Nov 24. And so maybe that's the key thing here. Pray and ask yourself what action feels right for you today—and how you can honor your choice and the program you attend at the same time.

Of course, if you have a sponsor, consider their suggestion. Hopefully it will be a suggestion or wisdom and not a direct command. Personally, my wisdom is this: If you think publicly announcing a relapse and starting at day 1 will derail your sobriety, then just don't. Just keep going. Just keep going and don't take chips and then someday if you decide to change your date, fine.

Your date is no one's business but your own. And the objections of others who might get upset if they knew—those objections are likely based on a certain kind of competitive spirit—*No fair!*

Love yourself and your recovery enough to be faithful to it first. Check your heart and your conscience. And of course, while it's fine that you keep your own and your sponsor's counsel, I don't recommend you lie. And maybe the most important thing I need to say is that it could be a big mistake *not* to publicly admit the slip, too—and if you keep relapsing, then it will be clear what you need to do.

In the meantime, if it's just silly pride about having relapsed, then bite the bullet.

As you know, we all only have one day at a time. I don't *have* a certain amount of years. I have *today.*

One last caution: It's almost always true that every time you relapse it becomes harder to get sober again. I've seen it over and over. People get casual about a relapse or think they'll just have a quick slip and get right back on the wagon—except they can't.

Some seed about the possibility of relapse gets planted and pretty soon they turn into chronic relapsers. And I don't know of any group of people on the planet more miserable. To enjoy few or none of the benefits of recovery while also not being able to enjoy drinking is to live in a nightmare. Don't go there, friend. Whatever you do. It might be life or death for you.

The Best Thing We Can Do

woke up thinking about two recent comments I read:

> *I just wonder if I will ever be able to forgive myself for hurting my closest friend. I have been a fool....drinking and talking... talking out of deep pain and having no idea what I was even saying....I am in recovery....but struggle with hating myself for hurting her.*

> *Oh, how I wish I could change the past & take my daughter's pain away. Alcoholism is such a cruel disease for the alcoholic & the one that have to endure the wrath it brings. All I could do was listen to her pain & let her express her anger towards me without becoming defensive. It hurt but I would do anything to help her to heal & being heard is important. What it's done to me is bring up tremendous guilt & shame."*

Dealing with broken relationships, guilt, and shame is by far one of the hardest things folks in recovery—from addiction, alcoholism, or just plain being human and selfish—have to deal with. Most of us arrive here sooner or later, though. Stricken with remorse, willing to change our ways, but stuck in an endless loop of regret.

Our recovery literature promises us that if we get sober and make amends eventually "we won't regret the past nor wish to shut the door on it." But most of us find it hard to not want to *slam* that door and escape the truth of how deeply we hurt others.

Of course, the irony is that if we *do* continue to wallow in guilt and regret, we're actually *more* likely to climb back into the same horrible behaviors that hurt people we love and made us so sorry in the first place. Why is that?

Because shame never set any one free. And because the meaning of forgiveness is to forgo taking vengeance. And if we are the person we need to forgive and we refuse to do that, we'll find a way—consciously or not—to take vengeance on ourselves through self-sabotage.

We'll be so tortured by our inability to let go of the past that we'll end up hating ourselves beyond what our soul can bear and eventually we'll be so desperate to escape our pain we'll decide we might as well drink or drug anyway, since we need relief and we clearly don't deserve sobriety. The condemnation of others and our own selves seems to prove this.

Here's another reason it's so hard to forgive ourselves. *We've bought into the lie that to feel guilty is somehow noble, a virtue, or proof of our repentance.* It's one of the most subtle but powerful lies in the universe: My own remorse and self-punishment can somehow pay the price for my mistakes and failures and the way I've wounded others.

But none of us can ever suffer enough to make up for how we hurt people. It's impossible. Only God can bridge that gap by his grace—and if we refuse to accept that grace, we take the path of Judas and self-destruction. We spread more pain.

I think that's the path my father took—he couldn't get over the mess he'd made of his life and all the wasted years and how he'd abandoned his own kids. I'm convinced it was part of what finally drove him to suicide.

All this to say, my heart breaks for the women who wrote those notes. They long not just to be forgiven, but to know how to forgive themselves. They long not just to make things right, but to have a key relationship restored.

Unfortunately, some relationships don't survive the ravages of how we fail each other in this life. Not because some of us are less worthy of forgiveness, but because some of us can't see beyond the wounds we've suffered.

I wish I had amazing advice for these readers, but mostly I want to just beg them to forgive themselves by faith. Piling on apologies doesn't usually help.

Continuing to try to prove your new intentions by groveling

doesn't help either. Instead, it just keeps the focus on our own guilty feelings and make us it all about us all over again. Our friend or mother or child or whoever we hurt is not moved by our self-pity.

The best thing we can do is set about to live in a way that proclaims the power of compassion and healing, that proves we've been set free from the past not because we're worthy but because the horrors of our mistakes forced us to discover in God a source of hope and mercy that is finally greater than our stubborn hearts can resist.

We can live in a way that bears witness to the understanding that every single one of us, believe it or not, has been doing the best we possibly can—given our own wounds, our past, what we know or don't, and the DNA we've been blessed/cursed with.

Few people are evil, I'm convinced. Most of us are just unhealed.

Yesterday I sat with an alcoholic in my office who had relapsed yet again and who was overcome with self-loathing. Determined to make it through the night sober, she wanted me to give her something to do when she got home. I told her I want her to ponder all the recent wreckage and havoc and insanity she's caused—and then write a letter to herself forgiving herself.

She broke into sobs. "I can do that," she said. "I want to do that."

Let's all do that today the best we can. And if you happen to be reading this and you're one of those folks whose been wounded too times to count by a very sick person like my friend or myself and you can't figure out how to forgive, I suggest the same exercise.

Start by forgiving yourself.

And because I love this poem so much I'm going to share it again: It's by the poet Hafiz:

Once a young woman said to me, "Hafiz, what is the sign of someone who knows God?"

I became very quiet, and looked deep into her eyes, then replied, "My dear, they have dropped the knife. Someone who knows God has dropped the cruel knife that most so often use upon their tender self and others."

Hearing Voices

Dave and I recently watched a show about a brilliant but terribly flawed FBI agent struggling with alcoholism (among other things).

At one point in the episode, her sister, who happens to be a doctor, says to her something like: "What's wrong with you is so wrong there's not even a diagnosis."

Ha! I thought this was such a funny line. Then I realized it was kind of familiar, too. It sounded exactly like the kind of thing the mean voice I hear in my head on a regular basis would say: *You're such a fraud and a failure! You're bad and broken in ways that go way beyond what it means to be a regular human.*

My sister has a lot of experience with this mean voice, too. Lately, she's been going to Alanon, which has been a great help to her—and me, too.

Last week, she called to tell me something she heard a woman say after a meeting that was so powerful to her she thought it might change her life.

Really? I thought. *A single idea could change your life?*

And then she told me what the woman said: "I'm single and I live alone, in an abusive relationship." Meaning, *with herself.*

Wow. My sister was right. This idea could change my life, too.

Of course, the notion that we're hard on ourselves is nothing new, but putting it in terms of being in a potentially abusive relationship is a fresh, helpful way to look at the importance of how we talk to and treat ourselves. Especially when you consider that, apart from God, the relationship we have with ourselves is the most constant, lasting, and influential one we'll ever have.

No wonder in recovery we emphasize self-care so much. Being in an abusive relationship with yourself is pretty much the definition of addiction, don't you think? So it goes to reason that healing this relationship would be a big part of what it takes to achieve long term recovery.

This was brought home to me in a real way yesterday when I got a call from a friend who's in the same treatment center I went to seven years ago. She, too, was asked to write a letter to herself about her alcoholism and how she intends to stay sober.

I'll never forget how much I cried and how surprisingly healing it was for me to write that letter. And it was the same for my friend. Something about intentionally talking to yourself in an encouraging, compassionate way makes you realize how much of the time you *un*intentionally talk to yourself in ways that bring you down.

So maybe it's worth asking questions like these more often: *If that voice in my head were incarnated into a person—what would our relationship look like? What do I put up with that I shouldn't? How might I set better boundaries about how I let myself think and behave toward myself?*

And since that voice in my head isn't about to reform or leave any time soon, *how can I respond to her in a way that doesn't just antagonize her further? How can I show that hurt, fear-driven part of myself the kind of compassion I'd show a sick friend?*

I need to think a lot more about this, and maybe you do, too. In the meantime, as we watch out for the mean voice in our head, we can also listen—with all our heart—for the voice of love that comes from our soul, created in God's image.

I hope you hear that voice often.

Inside
Every Monster

This past week, Dave has been out of town on a backpacking trip with his kids, and I have been taking care of business at home—which has included reorganizing my office (Okay the *re* part is a lie—it never was organized to begin with).

In the process, in the bottom of a drawer, I came across an old handwritten note from Dave. (So many women never receive a single such letter in their lives. I'm aware how fortunate I am.) I have a reason for sharing this. Here's the note—minus some goopy stuff.

> Heather, This is a love note to you. I love you with my whole heart. You interest me. You interest me more than any other woman. You are a continually unfolding gift to me. ...You impress me with your courage to face your life, and live it, and grow it to something you can't see now or hardly name. Good things are ahead for you and us, let us pursue and wait in faith together. I think a new Heather who was always there is walking out into the Light. It's not my life or my work, but I'm here—a witness. I'm lucky. Thank you for your love and your beauty. You grace me . . . I love you, Dave

It's an amazing letter, isn't it? But here's the shocking part. Dave always dates his notes—and this one is dated Feb 7, 2007. That's six weeks *before* my big surrender in March of that year when I finally *did* walk into the light, tell the truth about my alcoholism, and reach for help.

How on earth could my husband have written such a note during what were in retrospect the darkest days of our marriage and of my alcoholism? I drank to blackout almost every night. I physically attacked Dave in drunken rages and often woke up in the guest room. How could he have written that I "grace" him? How could I not even remember ever getting this letter?

Seven and a half years later, I think two things are true. Part of Dave must have sensed that I was nearing a breaking point, on the verge of a huge shift.

But more important, I now realize that it probably wouldn't have happened when it did if Dave hadn't done what he did in this note. Which was to see past my monsterish behavior to the hurting girl who was trapped inside. Which was to say to me, "I see you, Heather. I know you're in there. I know this isn't who you really are or what you really want. I believe in the better you."

By some miracle, my heart must have heard him, even if my head didn't know it. So I guess I'm sharing this note as a way of reminding you, and maybe inspiring you, that if it is at all possible (it might not be for you right now), one of the kindest and most powerful ways you can help an alcoholic or addict—or for that matter, *anyone* you love—is to look past the ugly actions that come from their wounded places and affirm the goodness of who they really are underneath. I think that's what Dave did for me.

Of course, loving a broken person toward their better self can seem like a herculean task. I so get that. But I know if Dave was here, and I showed him this note, he'd agree. With God's help, anything is possible.

And inside every monster is a miracle waiting to happen.

Made in the USA
Columbia, SC
25 January 2021